THE COMPLETE NIGHT OF THE LIVING DEAD FILMBOOK

JOHN RUSSO · **Coauthor of *NIGHT OF THE LIVING DEAD***
Preface by GEORGE ROMERO

HARMONY BOOKS / NEW YORK

THE COMPLETE NIGHT OF THE LIVING DEAD FILMBOOK
BY JOHN RUSSO

"Directors of the new high-budget horrors would do well to study the honest brutality and unrelieved gruesomeness of NIGHT OF THE LIVING DEAD; they might learn the difference between what makes people giggle nervously and what makes them scream in terror."
—Howard Smith, The Village Voice

BOOKS BY JOHN RUSSO
NIGHT OF THE LIVING DEAD
RETURN OF THE LIVING DEAD
THE MAJORETTES
MIDNIGHT
LIMB TO LIMB
BLACK CAT
BLOODSISTERS
THE AWAKENING
DAY CARE

Acknowledgements
Jaimie Aiello, Jim Aiello, James Aiello, Debra Ciarelli, Cinefantastique, Fred Clarke, Bill George, Michael Gornick, Lilo Guest, Karl Hardman, Image Ten Productions, Diana Michelucci, James Manzella, Joe Mavrodis, George Romero, Mary Lou Russo, Russ Streiner, Gary Surmacz, Dolores Wilt.

Concept and Interior Design: Robert V. Michelucci
Associate Design: Debra A. Ciarelli

Published by Harmony Books, a division of Crown Publishers, Inc., 225 Park Avenue South, New York, New York 10003
Originally published by Imagine, Inc., P.O. Box 9674, Pittsburgh, PA 15226
HARMONY and colophon are trademarks of Crown Publishers, Inc.
Manufactured in the United States of America

Library of Congress Cataloging-in-Publication Data
Russo, John, 1939—
  The Complete Night of the Living Dead filmbook.
  1. Night of the living dead. I. Title.
PN1997.N5215R87   791.43'72   86-329
ISBN 0-517-56170-0 (pbk.)

10 9 8 7 6 5 4 3 2 1
First Harmony Edition

This book is dedicated to the energetic and talented cast and crew of NIGHT OF THE LIVING DEAD.

Preface by George A. Romero Director of NIGHT OF THE LIVING DEAD

If you want to see what turns a B movie into a classic...don't miss NIGHT OF THE LIVING DEAD. It is unthinkable for anyone seriously interested in horror movies not to see it.

—Rex Reed

In 1968, the film industry was beginning to lose breath under the stranglehold of televideo growth. The precious ticket-buying dollar was no longer supporting Bergman or Fellini or even Doris Day. It was recognized that films had to be produced less expensively and promoted more carefully if they were to make money at the box office. The independent film distributor was becoming as significant a force as the major studio.

These circumstances opened the door of the industry to the independent filmmaker. Where he could not crack the shell of the Hollywood establishment, he could get the ear of a small independent distributor; and where the small distributor could not compete with *Quo Vadis* in the golden days, he could certainly fill empty screens as they became available. While escapism pap was being dished to the public in great, heaping, twenty-four hours-a-day bowlfulls on the tube, the exploiters of the big screen turned to violence, horror and sex.

In this context, the independent filmmaker had to become an investment banker and to sometimes be willing to compromise his art, but it was at least possible for him to work.

A group of us, friends since college, had been operating a commercial-production facility in Pittsburgh since 1961. All the while we were producing television commercials and industrial films, we were gloating over the fact that we had been making a profit and that we had accumulated a complement of equipment along with the technical know-how to fully service film production. We were completely self-contained. We had the capability to complete a feature film in our shop, The Latent Image, Inc.

Prior to the conception of *Night of the Living Dead*, we had tried, unsuccessfully, to generate interest in Pittsburgh's financial community in the viability of low-budget theatrical production. Frustrated by the negative response, we observed the happenings in the distribution field, and reasoned that an investment in a film designed to capitalize on the industry's confusion and thirst for the bizarre would be relatively safe, so we did the one thing that breaks the primary rule of any high-risk venturing: we put up our own money.

Ten of us, friends through simultaneous growth, formed a corporation called Image Ten and advanced the seed money to begin production. I had written a short story, an allegory inspired by Richard Matheson's "I Am Legend," which dealt with the mass return from the grave of the recently dead and their need to feed off the flesh and blood of the living. I was in the process of converting the idea to a shooting script, but was only half finished when the company was ready to begin shooting. John Russo took over the task of script-writing while we prepared to move to Evans City, Pennsylvania, and open our lenses.

All of us who were involved in the production of *Night of the Living Dead* thought of ourselves as total filmmakers. We all took turns loading magazines, gaffing, gathering and making props, shooting, recording, editing. We were all involved in the total process.

We cast the players from among friends, both vocational and avocational actors, entirely in Pittsburgh. From the beginning, the kismet-factors which were to ultimately pull the film on to a spectacular success as a classic in its genre began to accumulate. The casting of Duane Jones as the character of Ben was one of the first such factors. In the script, Ben was ill-defined. He had to be young, fit, powerful and cunning. We cast a black man not because he was black, but because we liked Duane's audition better than others we had seen. The socio-political implications of Ben's being black have been studied and pondered and written about in various journals, and it caused one critic in his exuberance to write that he heard the strains of "Ole Man River" in the music score when Ben meets his fate.

Perhaps *Night of the Living Dead* is the first film to have a black man playing the lead role regardless of, rather than because of, his color, and in that sense the observation of the fact is valid, but we did not calculate that this would be an attention-grabber. We backed into it. Our own relaxed, honest, uninhibited, naive attitudes as we approached the production ultimately read-out as unconscious elements in the picture which added to its realism, offhandedness and uniqueness.

Similarly, the use of black and white rather than color was a budgetary decision rather than an esthetic one. The allegory which is assigned to the film's message was not at all in our minds as we worked. Our way of thinking, however, led us away from formula, and the characters were not painted as heroic or exceptional in any way. The lead characters were hapless victims without redeeming subplot; the ghouls were banal in appearance, weak and conquerable as individuals but invincible in their sheer mass; the government officials, members of the press and avenging posses of ghoul-hunters were ineffectual blunderers who did not have absolute answers and ultimately resorted to trucking over the countryside with shotguns blasting out the zombies' brains. This method of destruction was singularly unpretentious. These factors all elevated the film from the ordinary, and because of its realistic presentation, an allegorical interpretation becomes possible.

I directed for naturalism and saw no reason to cut away for reaction shots when the ghouls began devouring the flesh of their victims. In fact I was delighted when one of our investors, who happened to be in the meat-packing business, turned up on the set with a sackful of animal innards which made the sequences seem so real, never realizing the extent of taboo-breaking the scenes would achieve.

Over and above all this, the film has a nostalgic quality which recalls the horror films and the E.C. comic books of the fifties.

And finally, *Night of the Living Dead* has some genuinely fine cinematic craftsmanship. That craftsmanship provides an audience with real, startling shocks and gut-felt, edge-of-the-seat terror as the story unfolds and the inescapable climax becomes more and more evident. The film opens with a situation that has already disintegrated to a point of little hope, and it moves progressively toward absolute despair and ultimate tragedy. Nobody comes riding in at the end with the secret formula that will save us all. The ghouls, in essence, win out.

When the film opened, it was met by outraged attacks against its motives, its competence of execution, and the unabashed saturation of gore. It was flagellated by critics and commentators who viewed it as a contributing factor to everything from crime in the streets to the corruption of the morals of American youth.

We watched, interestedly, as the clippings appeared across the country. We were sometimes disappointed and sometimes amused by the angry editorials we had provoked, but we realized they were proof that we had accomplished our goal. We had found our window of entry. We had finished a film and made it available for distribution at one of those magic moments in the competitive scramble for attracting an audience. *Night of the Living Dead* was produced for $114,000 (seed cash of $60,000, the rest deferred until after release), and it has grossed millions, appearing on the *Variety* charts of top-grossing films in both 1969 and 1970. It has been on screen, somewhere in the world, constantly since 1968. It has been translated into seventeen foreign languages and has a cult following worldwide. It was the film that originated the midnight screenings which are so popular nowadays. It has been invited into the Museum of Modern Art programs, and is respected by critics and buffs alike as possibly the best film of its type.

If you have gone to see *Night of the Living Dead*, I thank you.

From Pittsburgh,
the city of the first Nickelodeon,
George A. Romero

John Russo in ghoul make-up

JOHN RUSSO
CO-AUTHOR OF A HORROR CLASSIC

"If you do like horror films, this may well be the most horrifying ever made. It eschews comic relief, explanatory scientists, romance, distractions of any sort—all the conventional elements usually tacked on to horror films to relieve tensions and which usually merely dilute interest."
—Elliott Stein, Sight and Sound

John Russo learned the film business from scratch, following his graduation from West Virginia University (1961) where he majored in English and began writing short stories and screenplays. He started out to be a teacher and writer, but got sidetracked into a more flamboyant career by two friends, George Romero and Russell Streiner, who were operating a commercial film company in Pittsburgh. Romero and Streiner were later to become the director and co-producer, respectively, of NIGHT OF THE LIVING DEAD, while Russo and Romero shared screenwriting duties.

Russo says, "In those days we were known as a bunch of young, creative maniacs. We busted hump making literally hundreds of TV spots, sales films and documentaries— award-winning stuff on ridiculously low budgets. Our goal was to acquire skills that we could turn to good use if the opportunity ever came to make a full-length theatrical feature instead of films about ketchup, pickles, paint, beer, art schools, chemical cor- porations and political candidates. NIGHT OF THE LIVING DEAD was successful large- ly because of the insane zeal of all who work- ed on it. It was very much a group effort, with George Romero as leader. Everybody involv- ed had to be ready, able and willing to do almost anything and everything. We knew we were up against the wall, trying to make the best picture possible under adverse condi- tions, and we had to be bold and innovative every step of the way."

Sometimes being bold and innovative meant doing things that were zany or dangerous. John Russo not only helped write, film, edit, finance and market NIGHT OF THE LIVING DEAD; he also acted the part of a ghoul stabbed in the forehead with a tire iron, and let himself be set on fire, with a trail of gasoline going up his clothes—because the production couldn't afford a stuntman with an asbestos suit in a sequence filled with ex- ploding molotov cocktails.

Russo looks back upon those early days of youthful exuberance and camaraderie with fond nostalgia. They were days filled with hard work as well as good times, as he and his friends struggled to launch their careers as writers, actors and filmmakers. NIGHT OF THE LIVING DEAD turned out to be a major stepping stone, the one they were all hoping for, although they could hardly have antici- pated its magnitude.

Since then, John Russo has gone on to write, produce and/or direct three more movies and to publish a string of novels. Millions of fright fans know him as the perpetrator of macabre creations such as MIDNIGHT, BLOODSISTERS and THE AWAKENING. His latest horror novel, DAY CARE, will be published in March of 1985 by Pocket Books.

HOW NIGHT OF THE LIVING DEAD CAME TO BE
or
LET'S GET TOGETHER AND MAKE A MONSTER FLICK

"NIGHT OF THE LIVING DEAD wrings maximum effects from an ab-. solute minimum of means. Indeed, countless far more ambitious movies could benefit from such drive and vitality."
—Kevin Thomas, Los Angeles Times

On a snowy cold day in January 1967, George Romero, Richard Ricci and I were having lunch at Samreny's Restaurant on Market Street, around the corner from The Latent Image, Inc., the Pittsburgh-based film company operated by me and George, Vince Survinski, Larry Anderson, Russell Streiner and Russ's brother Gary.

Richard Ricci was an old friend of ours who had been discharged from the navy some months ago, and through George's influence had landed a job as a film producer for Ketchum, McLeod and Grove, Inc.—a large advertising agency. We at the Latent Image had been producing TV commercials for some of KM&G's smaller accounts, and we had imagined that Richard's placement in a position of responsibility might help us land some of their bigger-budget stuff. But this hadn't come to pass, and we were disgruntled. To our old pal, George and I let our disgruntlement be known.

Over grilled provolone sandwiches on Italian bread, and a few bottles of beer, Richard was trying to explain to George and me why he hadn't been able to help us much so far. Tall, dark and handsomely suave, he sucked on a filter-tip cigarette and let the smoke curl out through his nostrils. He had a habit of speaking in a low, tight voice that gave what he had to say a fine edge of drama that it didn't deserve.

"You guys know how it is. Everything the agency produces has to go through Rocco. He's *from* New York, and he likes to go back there to work. It makes him feel important. Being in Pittsburgh, for him, is like being in *exile*. He lets you do the small-budget stuff because he can't afford to go to The Big Apple with it, and he knows damn well you'll do a top-notch job. But as soon as he has big bucks to spend, he runs to New York where he can

hobnob with the high-priced talent and go see the Broadway shows."

Rocco Dellarso, about whom Richard was speaking, was the head of the Radio-TV Department of Ketchum, McLeod and Grove. He had been transferred to Pittsburgh from New York, where one of his claims to fame that he liked to boast about was coming up with the slogan for *Schaeffer's* beer: "The one beer to have when you're having more than one."

"Same old story," I grumped. "We only got $3,000 a spot for the Iron City Beer commercials we produced for Rocco last year, but they copped a bronze and a silver medal at the New York International Film Festival, competing against Stan Freberg stuff that cost over a hundred thousand dollars. But still it doesn't convince anybody we're good enough to handle big jobs."

"It *convinces* damn near *everybody*," Richard contradicted. "But the quality of your work is not the point. It's not even at issue. You're in a business where friendships, kickbacks and who's sleeping with whom very often decide where the big jobs go."

"Fuck it," George said. "It's a goddamn rat-race. We got into it in 1962 hoping it would pave the way to doing features. You know that, Richard."

"Yeah, but you've got to live in the meantime. You've got to pay your bills. I don't know how you guys at Latent Image manage to hang in."

"Me neither," I said, and took another gulp of beer. Like George, Russ and the other guys I worked with, I always had a stack of bills that I didn't know how I was going to pay; all of us were constantly harassed by creditors and collection agencies.

"We bought a 35-millimeter Arriflex camera with complete accessories last

Latent Image promo—cartoon by George Romero

They said that Young Rick
paid $700 to buy
Jesse James' guns...

He was payin' for the name,
and what he called
"Reliability."
He made out fine for awhile...

...til Sneaky Pete
blew hell out of 'im.
With an eight dollar scatter gun...
and a little creative ingenuity...

BAROOO

WE HAVE TO ADMIT THAT WE CAN'T TOUCH EIGHT DOLLARS, BUT WE USE CREATIVE INGENUITY TO BLOW HELL OUT OF HIGH PRICES, TOO... DURING THE PAST FIVE YEARS, FILMS PRODUCED BY THE LATENT IMAGE, INC. HAVE WON THIRTY SEVEN MAJOR AWARDS IN FESTIVAL COMPETITION. MORE THAN TWO DOZEN OF THESE WERE TELEVISION COMMERCIALS PRODUCED FOR $6,000 OR LESS, WHILE COMPETING SPOTS IN SOME CASES HAD BUDGETS IN EXCESS OF $50,000. WE'D LIKE TO SHOW YOU OUR REEL SO YOU CAN JUDGE FOR YOURSELF.

THE LATENT IMAGE, INC.

week," George said, smiling. "Used, it cost us $3500. All the bread we make goes into overhead and equipment. We barely draw enough salary to live on. Five years ago we had five hundred bucks and a piss-poor Bolex camera. Right now we have a complete studio—lights, cameras, recording, inter-locking, editing and mixing facilities—every-thing we need to make a feature motion pic-ture except the money to pay for filmstock and processing, actors, extras, sets, props, costumes, music and special effects."

"Go after some investment," Richard said brightly, as if it were as easy as falling off a log.

"We tried that," George said. "Pittsburgh money feels safe investing in iron foundries. You tell them you want to make a film, they want to beat you over the head and put you in a straight-jacket."

"Go out of town for money," Richard said. "Go to New York and Los Angeles, where they understand what you're doing."

"Understand, shit," George said. "Nobody in New York or L.A. believes anything but pig-iron can be made in Pittsburgh."

We all fell silent, thinking.

We didn't know it, but NIGHT OF THE LIVING DEAD was about to be born.

Nobody working at The Latent Image at that time really wanted to make TV commer-cials, except Larry Anderson, a former ad-agency account man. He and his wife Jeannie, who was our secretary-receptionist, would have been quite happy doing commercials from now till doomsday, if we could have found a way of making big money at it. Larry was the only one of our group who did not want to work on NIGHT OF THE LIVING DEAD, and he left the company soon after the picture was released.

Back in 1960 George Romero, Russ Streiner, Richard Ricci, Rudy Ricci (Richard's cousin) and an actor named Ray Laine had borrowed $2,000 from George's uncle and had formed a company called Ram Produc-tions, with ambitions of producing a feature movie in the shape of a series of comic vignet-tes, to be titled EXPOSTULATIONS. They bought a 16-millimeter Bolex camera and some filmstock, and enlisted legions of friends, such as me, to work crew, run errands and act in the picture. They actually got it all filmed and edited but it lacked narration and music and money to pay for a 35-millimeter blow-up. EXPOSTULATIONS, unfinished, remains in film cans at The Latent Image studio, to this day.

When Ram Productions disbanded in 1962 George Romero and Russ Streiner made some deals with the other parties involved so they could get to keep the Bolex camera. Richard Ricci enlisted in the navy. Ray Laine concentrated on acting. Rudy Ricci resumed studies at the University of Pittsburgh. I graduated from West Virginia University, taught school for almost a year, and got drafted. Before I departed for two years in the army, George and Russ told me they were going to start a commercial film company and if they were doing well by the time I got out, I could come to work with them. It sounded good to me, as I was enthralled with the idea of making films through the taste of it I had gotten while working on EXPOSTULATIONS.

I had met George Romero in 1957 through Rudy Ricci. Rudy and I had been friends since fourth grade, in the small iron-and-coke town where we both grew up—Clairton, Pennsylvania—fifteen miles south of Pittsburgh. When Rudy enrolled in Carnegie Institute of Technology (now Carnegie-Mellon University) to study art, he met George Romero, a fellow freshman, and they became close friends. Later, Ray Laine, Richard Ricci and Russell Streiner became part of the group—they were studying acting and stage production at the University of Pittsburgh and the Pittsburgh Playhouse School of the Theater. I was a student at West Virginia University at this time, and could only be part of the group's activities during vacations.

In 1957 all of us were about 18 years old, except Ray Laine who was a few years older. We each had big dreams of becoming successful actors, writers or film producers and directors. The dreams were fueled by George Romero, a big, likeable, talented, secretly shy boy away from home for the first time and bent on impressing his new group of friends.

George was from New York and he talked confidently about films, film equipment and production techniques. His knowledge of these things was actually pretty sketchy, but he knew enough to impress *us*. In the summer preceding the start of his college days, he had worked as a gopher (go for this, go for that) on the set of BELL, BOOK AND CANDLE starring Kim Novak and Ernie Kovacs. He had won a prize for an 8-millimeter film he made when he was in high school. And his father was a New York artist, specializing in the creation of film posters and other promotional material. It is easy to see now how George as a small boy must have gotten hooked on the thrills and fantasies of motion pictures, from being inside his father's studio, surrounded by luridly dramatic stills, banners, press books and one-sheets.

It was George's drive and enthusiasm that

led to the formation of Ram Productions and our quixotic effort at launching ourselves into the big time with a comedy called EX-

POSTULATIONS, produced on a mere $2,000. In the summer of 1960 when this fateful step was taken, we were all about to graduate from college, and I suppose we each had secret fantasies of succeeding beyond anyone's wildest hopes and never having to go to work in corporation land. Even today it seems something of a miracle that we actually completed the filming of EXPOSTULATIONS, and some of the bits aren't bad.

Anyway, in 1962 George and Russ went into business with a Bolex camera and an additional five hundred bucks borrowed from George's uncle. They got a store-front flat in an impoverished section of Pittsburgh known as the South Side. Rent was fifty dollars a month. George, an excellent painter and sculptor, made a large and beautiful bas-relief sign advertising the name of the new company, The Latent Image. The sign was the nicest thing about the place. Inside there were a few sticks of Goodwill furniture. There either wasn't any heating system, or else it didn't work—I forget which—and on some winter mornings George and Russ had to chip ice out of the commode bowl before they could flush it. They ate, slept, worked and played at "the studio." A few jobs came in, which involved taking still photographs of babies, or people getting married.

Part of the proceeds from these meager jobs was used to buy a big hockey game and a pet monkey. When there wasn't any work, which was ninety-eight percent of the time, George and Russ would sit just inside the plate glass window playing hockey, intently twisting and pulling levers to make the tin players swat at the puck. Sometimes they would borrow money to eat, or to feed the monkey or take him to the veterinarian. Other times all three—George, Russ and the monkey—went for days without eating.

I forget how it came about, but Larry Anderson brought them their first "big job." Larry was working for an advertising agency at the time, and he had to produce a commercial for the Buhl Planetarium sky show. The commercial had to show a spaceship landing on the moon. There was plenty of money to work with—$1600. Clearly not enough to actually go to the moon and film it. Could it be done on a tabletop in a storefront in South Side with water frozen in the commode bowl?

It could. Russ and George painted glowing pictures for Larry, their brains feverish with lust for the sixteen-hundred greenbacks the job promised—which was a lot more than the twenty-five bucks they had gleaned for their last series of baby pictures.

Rudy Ricci's brother Mark was majoring in math and science at Carnegie Tech. He and his friends had built their own radio-controlled rockets large enough and sophisticated enough to shoot over a mile into the air, with mice in their nosecones. Mark's aid was donated gratis to the project. George did all the backdrops and related artwork. Russ helped, molding the surface of the moon out of clay.

The Buhl Planetarium spot was wildly successful. The lunar-landing effect turned out as well as most such depictions in science-fiction features. Through Larry Anderson's efforts, his client paid to have the finished commercial blown up and shown as a "filler" during intermissions at drive-in theaters in the Pittsburgh area.

Russ and George lost money on the job. But it made getting additional work a little easier. And in 1965, shortly before I came to work with them, they were able to get a small-business loan of $30,000 (co-signed by George's uncle) which enabled them to move into The Latent Image's present headquarters in downtown Pittsburgh. Things still weren't easy. When I started working there, learning the film business from scratch, I was supposed to be getting paid $325 per month. Russ and George were each getting $400. But this was theoretical. We often went without getting paid for months at a time, sleeping on the studio floor, borrowing from friends and finance companies and working as hard as we could on the few jobs that came in, doing our best on them though they never seemed to quite pay the bills. Yet we couldn't bid the work higher, or we simply wouldn't get it; it would go to New York.

A Latent Image press kit photo of Russo

14

Little by little, some progress was being made, though it was hard to discern when we were in the middle of it. By 1967 we were fully equipped. Our pitch to clients was that we were "a full-service film production company, from script to finished print." We had learned much, by working on everything from TV commercials about beer, pickles and suntan lotion to longer films about political candidates, advertising agencies and toilet bowl cleaners. The pace was insane. Through winter and early spring we would get no work at all, and then it would all come in at once. Many times George, Russ and I had gone without sleep for three and four days at a stretch—filming, editing, producing certain jobs and driving from one location to another throughout Pennsylvania, Ohio and West Virginia.

We had gotten a reputation in some circles of being an energetic nucleus of creative maniacs who could make good films for those who couldn't afford—or didn't want—to spend very much money. We were fiercely proud of our work. But most of the time we were broke, frustrated, and physically and mentally exhausted.

We were ripe to try a daring move which might break us out of the rat-race and into clear sailing.

I suggested it to George and Richard that day in Samreny's Restaurant.

"We have all the gear," I said, thinking out loud. "Suppose all of us at Latent Image got together—plus a few friends, like Richard—and each of us kicked in six hundred dollars. If we had ten people, that would make six thousand dollars. Could we make any kind of feature-length film on that?"

George's eyes lit up. Richard let cigarette smoke curl out through his nostrils.

"That's four thousand dollars more than we had to make EXPOSTULATIONS," I said as follow-up. "And we didn't have our own cameras, lights, editing equipment and mixing gear back then. Finishing the sound track would be the least of our worries."

"We'd never afford a finished print on that kind of money," George said. "The most we could do is buy filmstock, maybe process and work-print it—if it was in black-and-white." His voice took on added enthusiasm while he was talking; there was nothing that could light George up like the prospect of making a movie.

"You guys are crazy," Richard said, grinning widely as he leaned back and stubbed his butt out in the ashtray.

But George and I were off and running. I kept pushing, not wanting the idea to lose momentum. "George, we could finish the editing and the mix, and we'd have an interlock. If it was good enough, we could decide then how to come up with bread to get a 35-millimeter print. Maybe we could sell the picture on the basis of the interlock. Or at least shake additional investment loose."

"What kind of film could you make on six thousand dollars?" Richard said scornfully. "Christ—it costs more than that to make a beer commercial."

"How about a monster movie?" I said. "We ought to be able to make something more legitimately terrifying than these things about giant praying mantises or creatures in rubber masks. I don't know what our film will be. We'll need a good strong concept that doesn't require much in the way of special effects."

Continental's publicity gimmick

Kyra Schon as a lovely young woman, ordinary child and a ghoul

George added, "Something contemporary. A story that takes place now. We use existing locations, and don't get hung into period costumes or sets."

"I repeat, you fucking guys are crazy!" Richard said.

George turned to me, his eyes gleaming. "Who would be the ten people to put up the six hundred bucks?"

I thought about it, and talked while I was thinking. "Well, we'll have to give each investor a piece of the action. But we want more out of them than just money—we want services. We shouldn't ask anybody in unless he or she can contribute strongly to the project—as an actor, sound engineer, lighting man—"

"We're going to need a lawyer," Richard broke in. "We'll probably have to set up a corporation."

George and I both laughed.

"What do you mean, we?" George asked Richard. "I thought you just said Jack and I were crazy."

(My name is John but Jack is my nickname. Most of my friends call me Jack.)

"I'm in," Richard said, in his low, tight, dramatic voice. "Christ, I'm in. This whole fucking thing will probably turn into a fiasco."

"We're going to make a movie!" George yelled, and banged his fist on the tabletop so hard that the bottles, glasses and ashtrays rattled.

All the customers in the bar heard him and turned to gawk at us. But we were laughing and ordering more beer, doping out the initial details of our big venture.

After washing down our provolone sandwiches with a few more bottles of beer, Richard went back to work at Ketchum and George and I walked around the corner to The Latent Image to talk things over with the rest of the people in the company. On the way, from the time we left the restaurant, George began getting more and more worried, till his "up" mood had vanished as if it never existed.

"Larry will never go for it," he said mournfully. "Neither will Russ, Vince...maybe. Gary is no problem. Yudell will probably thumb the whole thing."

George was talking about his Uncle Monroe Yudell, who had co-signed the $30,000 loan and had stock in The Latent Image which gave him a powerful voice in all company decisions till the loan was paid off.

"I think Russ will want in," I said. "I'm not worried about Larry—we don't really need him. I don't know about Vince and of

Vince Survinski & Jackie Faust preparing a meal for the crew

17

John Russo, Duane Jones, Harold Marenstein & Russ Streiner at the New York Premiere

course you're the one who has to deal with your uncle."

We got off the elevator on the fifth floor and saw Russ Streiner standing by the little table in the hall, pouring himself a cup of coffee. Jeannie Anderson was behing her receptionist's desk. Russ' brother Gary was in the reception area leafing through a magazine.

"Where's Larry?" I asked Jeannie.

"Lunch with a client. He's making a sales pitch on some bank spots."

"What's goin' on?" Gary asked, realizing something was up from the looks on our faces.

"We're going to make a feature movie—a monster flick," I said, laughing.

"Oh yeah?" Gary said, grinning. "I guess somebody came up to you two guys at lunch and gave you a lot of bread."

"I'm serious," I said. "Come on into Russ' office and we'll talk about it.

Jeannie was looking at us and shaking her head, exasperated at all the foolish nonsense we could get into when there wasn't money

to pay the rent.

George, Gary and I each got a cup of coffee and followed Russ in and he sat behind his desk. George and Gary took the remaining two chairs and I remained standing. George and I told our plan for coming up with six thousand dollars.

"I'd be in," Gary said immediately. "I think I can get the bread from my mother."

"If you get it from her, where will I get it?" Russ said.

"I think I'm going to borrow mine from a finance company," I told him. "Maybe you can too."

"I don't know where I'm getting mine either," George said. "I have to talk to Yudell, and he might put a stop to the whole thing."

"Well, this afternoon I'll work out some costs," Russ said. "I doubt if we can do it on six thousand. We'll probably need more—how much more, I don't know. But I'll be able to tell you before the afternoon is over."

By five or six o'clock that evening, it was determined that Russ, Gary and Vince Survinski wanted in on the project. Larry Anderson didn't. He made a big effort to talk us out of it, saying that he liked the idea of chipping in money, but if we did we ought to use it to "make a sixty-second spot that's a real mother—something that will knock the eyes off all the agency producers and help us land some big-budget jobs."

Larry was serious about this, but the rest of us couldn't help laughing. We never really wanted to make commercials; we were looking for a way out of doing them. Larry didn't fit in with the group, and his notion of making "a sixty-second spot that's a real mother" was to us pathetically ironic and ludicrous.

Russ had some bad news for us. He figured that we couldn't do any kind of 35-millimeter feature film on less than twelve thousand dollars—double the six thousand we had been talking about. This knocked the wind out of everybody's sails and we stood or sat or paced around in the reception area, numbed to silence.

"Well, okay," I said optimistically. "So each of the ten has to bring in one additional investor."

"Twenty people!" Russ exclaimed. "We'd have the pie cut up so many ways that if the picture did make any money we wouldn't see shit out of it."

"Wait a minute," I argued. "The first ten people are going to contribute both money and services. They deserve more stock than the second ten, who put up only money."

"That could work," George said. "We'll have to check with a lawyer to make sure it can legally be done that way."

"Who are the first ten?" Russ asked.

We talked it over and came up with the following list, all of whom (some requiring more persuasion than others) eventually accepted our offer and became the first ten investors in our new feature motion picture production company, which we called Image Ten, Inc.:

George A. Romero—director, cinematographer

Russell W. Streiner—producer

John A. Russo—writer, assistant cameraman

Vincent D. Survinski—production manager

Gary R. Streiner—recording and mixing

Richard Ricci—actor, friend

Rudy Ricci—actor, friend

Karl Hardman—co-producer

Marilyn Eastman—actress, production assistant

Dave Clipper—attorney

Karl Hardman and Marilyn Eastman were partners in Hardman Associates, Inc., a sound studio specializing at that time in the produc-

John & Mary Lou Russo with Keith Wayne at the World Premiere

19

tion of industrial shows and radio commercials. We had cast them in a number of television commercials and had gotten to know them fairly well. Both were good actors and had other talents we felt would be valuable, plus a capable staff to back them up and help with production details. We knew they were good enough to play key roles in our proposed motion picture, which would save us quite a bit of money and guarantee at least two top-quality performances. They had a library of music at Hardman Associates which eventually contributed heavily toward the sound track of NIGHT OF THE LIVING DEAD, as did their work with special music and sound effects that they invented on their own. Karl Hardman was so effective in helping to organize the production and bringing in additional investors that Russ Streiner offered to share the "producer" credit with him.

George Romero's uncle, Monroe Yudell—a New York doctor—did not turn out to be as tough to deal with as George had anticipated. Yudell did insist, however, that The Latent Image, Inc. should retain a 20% fee for providing the production services, equipment and facilities for the project. We all agreed to

this.

In a meeting with Attorney Dave Clipper, we decided that Image Ten, Inc. would be set up with an option of selling one hundred shares of stock. The first ten investors would each get six shares for six hundred dollars; the next ten investors would get only two shares for six hundred dollars. That would leave us twenty shares to sell, in case we needed to raise additional capital at some time in the future. The Latent Image was not to be a shareholder; it would be paid 20% of the gross profits of the picture, if there were any.

We also agreed—and later it turned out to have been a critical decision—that Image Ten would be chartered to make only one feature motion picture. This was our way of guaranteeing the investors that we wouldn't tie up any profits by sinking them into a new project that some of the group might not approve of. In other words, if our very first venture made money, we would be obliged to pay it out to the risk-takers who had supported us.

George Romero was elected president of Image Ten; Russ Streiner, vice-president; Vince Survinski, treasurer. I was elected secretary.

We had everything we needed except ten additional investors and a good script that could be filmed on twelve thousand dollars.

Vince Survinski, our capable and efficient treasurer, production manager and keeper of files and records, had made a job envelope for the Image Ten project, as was his habit to do for each and every job as soon as he got wind of it. He wrote a job number on the envelope and a job title: MONSTER FLICK. That was the way the feature was known all through pro-

duction. Our first finished 35-millimeter print bore the title, NIGHT OF THE FLESHEATERS, but we had to change it when we got threatened by a lawyer whose clients had already made a picture by that name. The next title was NIGHT OF ANUBIS— George's brainchild—*Anubis* being the Egyptian god of death. It wasn't until the picture was ready for release by The Walter Reade Organization that it was given its final title, NIGHT OF THE LIVING DEAD.

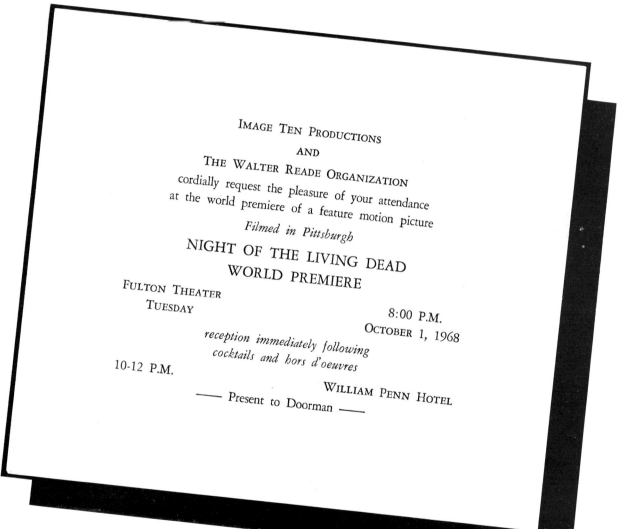

IMAGE TEN PRODUCTIONS

AND

THE WALTER READE ORGANIZATION

cordially request the pleasure of your attendance
at the world premiere of a feature motion picture

Filmed in Pittsburgh

NIGHT OF THE LIVING DEAD
WORLD PREMIERE

FULTON THEATER
TUESDAY

8:00 P.M.
OCTOBER 1, 1968

*reception immediately following
cocktails and hors d'oeuvres*

10-12 P.M.

WILLIAM PENN HOTEL

—— Present to Doorman ——

Pittsburghers Steal A Scene From Hollywood Movie Moguls

By WILLIAM H. WYLIE
Press Business Editor

There's a little bit of Hollywood in Pittsburgh.

And that's not a reference to Gene Kelly, Adolph Menjou or William (Thin Man) Powell — natives who made it big at Holly-

FALSE STARTS:
THE MOVIES WE ALMOST MADE

"Now, about the film. The money was there. The equipment, too. I could see every frame, every character move, down to the blink of an eye. I could hear every word, every sound, every rustle of paper on the sidewalk. We had a reading of it. George almost shit nickles and so did everybody else. But the German wanted to direct. His ideas and mine were as different as sausages and elephants. We threw him out on his can. Ever since, he's been seeing his lawyer and doing strange little things, trying to worm his way back in."
—Rudy Ricci, in a letter to John Russo, Dec., 1963

Rudy Ricci wrote me the letter from which the above is an excerpt when I was in the army at Fort Bragg, North Carolina, wishing I could be back home to work with my friends on a movie called, THE FLOWER GIRL, for which Rudy had written the script. It was one of our numerous attempts over the years that for one reason or another never got off the ground.

In this case, "the German," a refugee from East Germany named Aberhardt Rollick, had wandered into The Latent Image with a burning desire to make himself famous via the silver screen. THE FLOWER GIRL was going to depict how he had escaped from a concentration camp. We were never quite certain that this had actually happened. Rollick had already been on the Jack Paar Show and a few other TV programs telling his rather fantastic life story, which could never be documented because according to him all his personal records and documents had been burned by the communists. He claimed to have been a stage and film director prior to his interment, but of course this was unsubstantiated.

When he fell out with George, Rudy and Russ, he blew some of the movie money he had raised by buying himself a new car and some expensive rugs and furniture, but a few years later he did manage to make a terrible film with some other group of people. I remember a scene that showed actors supposedly hanging by their thumbs from the rafters of a cell—except their arms were bent instead of stretched by their body weight, and they were conversing with no strain whatsoever, as if they were waiting for a bus. They were obviously standing on boxes, hatching their big escape plan.

When it came time to make our Monster Flick, we had no shortage of experiences like THE FLOWER GIRL to remind us of how easily our skyrockets could explode on the launching pad. Everytime we failed, skeptical relatives, parents and acquaintances would go tee-hee or tsk-tsk, shaking their heads dolefully or smirking at the "proof" that we were what they thought we were: little boys who would never grow up. We gave them plenty of "proof" that we would never learn "how to make a buck."

I already mentioned EXPOSTULATIONS, which actually got filmed and edited on a budget of $2,000, but never got a soundtrack.

Even before that, we were making little eight-millimeter movies that could never hope to go anywhere. George Romero was absolutely wild about movies—wilder than any of the rest of us—and he started making them sooner than any of us, too. At age fourteen he headed a group called Herald Pictures in New York City, which was an association of young filmmakers with adult advisers. Herald produced two little adventure films, GORILLA and MAN FROM THE METEOR. Then, when George was at Suffield Academy he won a prize for the film called EARTH-BOTTOM, for which he was made a member of Future Scientists of America. I don't think he ever aspired to be a scientist. He's one of the most talented, creative people I've ever known. He could have excelled as a novelist, actor, sculptor or painter—but making movies is what he loved to do best so it was where he put his energy. All through the early days at Latent Image, I was amazed at the marvelous things he could do with a camera —and he was perhaps even better as an editor.

Rudy Ricci and I grew up together, attended the same high school, and used to make a few eight-millimeter movies, too. They'd usually be "rumble" movies or some such nonsense. We'd get a bunch of friends together and we'd "star" as young hoods in a teenage gang fight. It was pretty amateurish stuff. But I think most of us imagined we could be the next James Dean or Sal Mineo in some copycat version of REBEL WITHOUT A CAUSE.

It wasn't until Latent Image got going, and George Romero and Russ Streiner had been in business a couple of years, with the rest of us helping out on the side, that the group slowly acquired enough expertise to make films that were truly professional. I was behind everybody else because of getting drafted into the army. I was itching to get out and catch up. It seemed like I was really missing out on all the great, exciting things I yearned to do in life. And my urge to get back into the real action was fired to a fever pitch by passages like this one from another letter from Rudy Ricci to me, written in September, 1963:

"George is the same weight, is running a growing business, is wearing Brooks Brothers suits, is talking Madison Avenue during the day and acting out his madness in the evenings as an escape, is ascending vertically into the tongue-wag-money-world-of-green-smelling-success. Is brandishing a cigar (his sword and shield). Has a staff working for him. Has a Volksbus to carry equipment. The business is flying up as rapidly as any business could—it might even be breaking speed records..."

Well, when I got out of the army in April, 1964, I found out that things weren't as peachy as they had seemed through Rudy's eyes. It was true that The Latent Image was a going concern, but it was a far cry from making anybody rich. Two new guys had joined the full-time staff—Larry Anderson and Bill Hinzman. Hinzman was a lighting specialist and still photographer. Later, he played the part of the ghoul who killed Johnny in the cemetery in the opening scene of NIGHT OF THE LIVING DEAD.

While I had been gone, a number of exciting things had been done besides a raft of television commercials and industrial films. One of these was a campy version of HARD DAY'S NIGHT, starring Russ, Rudy, Larry and Bill in Beatles' wigs. Another was a movie synched to Ken Nordine's JAZZMATAZZ—from his famous "Word Jazz" albums. And there was an "old-time movie"—a hilarious depiction of the move of The Latent Image from the pitiful South Side flat to spanking new headquarters in downtown Pittsburgh. These short films were done on a lark, just to keep the creative juices flowing. They sucked up all the profits from commercial work; and

they were "justified" by being edited into The Latent Image's presentation reel, used to help land new clients—if they weren't too "square" to be frightened away for good by some of the zanier stuff.

At about this same time, another opportunity to make a full-length feature reared its head. I got back from Fort Bragg just in time to be part of the preproduction and casting sessions. The movie was to be called WHINE OF THE FAWN, and Rudy Ricci was writing it, based on an earlier screenplay by George Romero. It was to be an "art film" and I guess it could be said that the concept was vaguely reminiscent of Bergman's THE VIRGIN SPRING. The story was set in 15th century England, and was about young people caught in the turmoil of religious wars and witchcraft persecution. It was a good property, and I think it would be a worthwhile project to produce, even today. Coincidentally, while Rudy had been writing it, I had started writing a novel based on the medieval witchcraft trials, and I turned over my research notes so he could make use of them.

Another striking sidelight on WHINE OF THE FAWN is that Tom Savini, the famous make-up and special effects expert, was a candidate for one of the lead roles, a young boy named Torin. Years later, because of remembering Tom from the WHINE OF THE FAWN casting sessions, George Romero gave him a chance to work on his vampire film, MARTIN. Now, of course, movie fans know Tom for his great effects in movies like FRIDAY THE 13TH, DAWN OF THE DEAD, CREEPSHOW and, currently, George Romero's DAY OF THE DEAD.

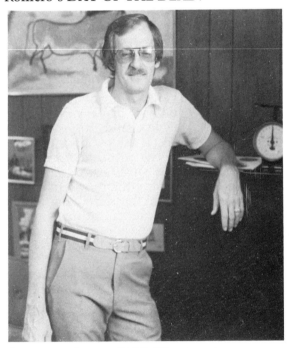

A recent photo of Bill Hinzman

24

Hinzman as the cemetery ghoul attacking Johnny

WHINE OF THE FAWN was to have been financed by the scion of a wealthy family of Pittsburgh merchants. He had impeccable credentials. But he never lived up to his promises. With the production almost ready to lens, he walked away and never came back. We couldn't even find him; he seemed to have disappeared. We heard rumors that he had suffered some sort of nervous breakdown, which may have meant that he was institutionalized somewhere, for all we knew. But we never found out for sure.

Naturally I had looked forward to working on WHINE OF THE FAWN. It would have been the biggest thing in my life up to that point. But, with its collapse, we all went back to scrambling for a living. I got a job teaching English and Science in my hometown, Clairton, Pa., and tried to help out with some of The Latent Image's commercial gigs on the side.

About a year later, in 1965, George Romero asked me to come and work with him full-time, after Bill Hinzman had resigned. George said he could pay me what I had been making as a teacher, which wasn't very much. It didn't matter to me—it was a dream come true. What did matter, and had me worried, was that I hadn't had nearly so much exposure to the technical aspects of filmmaking as George, Russ and Larry had at this time.

I said, "There must be dozens of guys in town who know more about cameras, lighting and sound gear than I do."

"Yeah, but that's *all* they know," George answered. "You can train a monkey to point a camera, but without creative ability, it doesn't matter."

"Okay," I agreed. "I'll come to work at Latent Image. But if I find out I can't hack the technical stuff, you won't have to fire me, I'll quit on my own."

Meanwhile, just before I started working there, Vince Survinski and Gary Streiner had joined the staff. Vince was our brash, colorful, enthusiastic "elder statesman," having fought in World War II and operated a roller rink before getting into the film business. He was always working his head off, not getting enough credit for all that he had a hand in, just being content to be the kind of guy who's invaluable to any production even if most of his work is behind the scenes. Gary Streiner, as I said before, was Russ's younger brother. Still in high school when he started working with us, he developed into one of the best sound engineers and sound mixers I've ever seen.

I learned quickly, too, as it turned out, and got to be a proficient cameraman, editor, gaffer, what-have-you. I found myself working harder than I had ever worked in my life. The first two and a half years after I joined the staff were probably the heaviest years of commer-

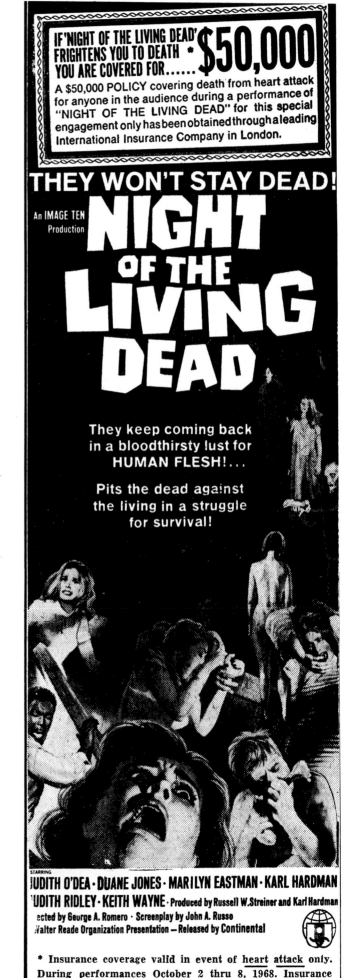

26

cial film production at The Latent Image. Dozens of gigs fell our way and somehow got cranked out even when they overlapped. Many times we would go three and four days with no sleep at all—filming, editing, building sets, making props, and driving to and from locations all over the eastern United States. We learned by doing, and doing, and doing. We had tremendous esprit de corps. We felt there was nothing we couldn't tackle and do well. Recognition started to come our way, too. Our walls were covered with awards we had won for our work—gold and silver medals and certificates from the New York International Film Festival, the Visual Communications Society, the Golden Reel, and the International Quorum of Motion Picture Producers.

Our reputation was made with low-budget stuff competing with—and beating—productions done for thousands of dollars more.

So, by the time the Monster Flick idea came along, we had cut our teeth and paid our dues. We weren't fly-by-nights off on a fluke. We were used to making purses out of sows' ears. We had the talent and qualifications, as a group, to make something big out of something that, in most people's eyes, had no right to happen at all.

George Romero & Gary Streiner filming Judy O'Dea

THE MONSTER FLICK SPLUTTERS AND COMES ALIVE

"Director George A. Romero has done an admirable job of creating hysteria and crude, brutal mayhem, with the most functional camerawork and sound. I think the makers of NIGHT OF THE LIVING DEAD set out like many before them to make a quick horror film for a quick profit and they probably will."

—Joseph Lewis, The Point

After I started working at The Latent Image, the way things panned out was that George and I developed a much closer friendship than we had had before, loafed around together, fed each other's hopes and enthusiasms, and put in longer hours at the studio than anyone else—because in those days he did most of the editing and I would do the conforming: matching the original camera footage to the edited work-print. Everybody else worked like hell, too, but George and I were the ones who stuck around at the studio even when we didn't have to. We were the zealots, the idea men, the ones who kept pushing for bolder and bolder moves to break us into the clear.

Russ Streiner was the detail man, the executive producer, with a good head for facts, figures and budgeting—and pitching clients and investors. I really admired his abilities in those areas.

What made George Romero a leader, though, without even trying, was that he was enormously likeable, of course talented, and with an uncanny ability to make others want to work with him and give their all. He didn't even realize what a natural leader he was. My function a lot of the time was to keep him psyched up with pep talks and fresh slants on things.

Once Image Ten was incorporated, we wanted to keep the momentum going, so the Monster Flick wouldn't fall on the scrapheap like so many other projects before it. We knew we needed a good script to keep the fire burning under everybody, and there was hardly any time to write one because we were swamped with commercial jobs that we needed to grind out for our bread and butter. Rather than let the project die of inertia, whenever we could scrape a few free hours out of an evening, we'd gather our friends together and sit on the floor of our screening room, drinking beer, smoking cigarettes, and bashing around story ideas.

There were two concepts that were bandied about that contained elements that eventually, whether subconsciously or on purpose, found their way into NIGHT OF THE LIVING DEAD.

The first concept—one that we all liked—was about monsters from outer space—only it was going to be a horror *comedy* instead of a horror drama. Some teenagers "hotrodding" around the galaxies were going to get involved with teenagers from earth, befriending them, while cartoon-like authority figures stumbled around, trying to unearth "clues" to the crazy goings-on. The outerspace teenagers were going to have a weird, funny pet called The Mess—a live garbage disposal that looked like a clump of spaghetti; you just tossed empty pop cans, popsicle sticks or whatever into The Mess and it ate them. There was also going to be a wacky sheriff called Sheriff Suck, who was totally inept and kept being the butt of all the teenagers' jokes.

HOLDING OVER! BREAKING ALL RECORDS! THANKS TO THOSE WHO MADE THIS RECORD-BREAKING ENGAGEMENT POSSIBLE. AND OUR APOLOGIES TO THE THOUSANDS WHO WERE TURNED AWAY THIS PAST WEEKEND.

IF 'NIGHT OF THE LIVING DEAD' FRIGHTENS YOU TO DEATH $50,000 YOU ARE COVERED FOR.... A $50,000 POLICY covering death from heart attack

I actually started to write a script for this idea late one night after George and I had finished with some film editing, and he was sitting at one typewriter and I at another, in the Latent Image orfices. Here are the first two pages—the opening scene—which contains ghouls and tombstones—elements that were used in a different way in NIGHT OF THE LIVING DEAD:

It is a night with many stars, and the sound of crickets. The universe is an inverted globe of stars and galaxies that engulf your eyes as the CAMERA PANS DOWN. There is only vast quietness, and the myriad pinpoint lights in the black, globular heaven.

CONTINUE THE LONG PAN DOWNWARD toward the surface of the earth. Something looms...stark and white: a tombstone. PAN AWAY, and there are myriad tombstones all around. The crickets still sing. The trees are stark and naked. The grave markers jut lopsidedly, whitely, from the crabgrass earth. They are as white and naked as picked bones; the moonlight lends an almost luminous shimmer—the pallid radiance of death.

A branch cracks. There is a rustle...and a faint footstep. Then, sounds of labor and heavy breathing become more intense. Amidst rustling and cracking of dead branches, two figures break out of the surrounding woods and into the clear of the cemetery.

The laboring figures are silhouettes, with the tombstones, against the starlit sky—but they are dark and the stones are white. One of the figures appears hump-backed. Both have odd shapes, as though they are not quite human. Between them they carry a box. They lay down their burden, and one turns, so that moonlight strikes his face: it is the fiendish face of a ghoul. His teeth are long and sharp, his eyes bulging, veins popping weblike from his forehead and cheeks. His frosty breath creeps around him and floats upward...

...as CAMERA PANS UP to...the stars. Suddenly there is an eerie electronic sound. A spherical luminous object whisks into frame, disappearing in the distance, in the depths, of the blackness and the pinpoints of light.

CUT TO our ghoul. We see his hideous face, while VOICEOVER we hear the question that his crony is asking.

CRONY: (startled) What was *that*, man?

The crony, too, looks like a ghoul, as in a MEDIUM SHOT we CUT TO him staring up at the sky. But his voice seemed high-pitched, like that of a teenage boy. We CUT BACK to the first ghoul. His face is startlingly changed. He is a boy. His rubber mask is in his hand.

GHOUL #1: (mutters) I dunno...a shooting star?

The second ghoul takes off his mask, too. He is another boy. Both stare at the sky a while longer. Then they kneel beside the box they were carrying, and open it. The first ghoul pulls out a bottle of beer. The second one takes it and pops it open. They both giggle. Another bottle is pulled out and popped open.

GHOUL #1: (chortling gleefully) Maybe someday Sheriff Suck will learn not to cool his beer on his back porch!

THE NEWS-TRIBUNE, BEAVER FALLS, PA., TUESDAY, JULY 2, 1968   PAGE 24

Evans City a Real Ghost Town

Zombies, Ghoul Friends Have Ball at Gass House

By DAVE BENARD

Barbara and her brother Johnny drive into the Willard Cemetery at dusk to place a wreath on their father's grave. A rumpled stranger approaches and without provocation, attacks them, leaving Johnny lying unconscious. Barbara flees in terror to a nearby farmhouse with the stranger following. That's how it all started about a year

said, "told me he remembered the farmhouse as a youth when he visited Evans City frequently and now wanted permission to use it in a movie."

After giving permission to the firm, Gass said they returned on July 7 and began filming. "They had a ball," Gass said. "They filmed almost every night until 2 or 3 a.m. I was going to tear the farmhouse down anyway so I let them do it for

Although Mr. and Mrs. Smith did not utter a word during the movie, they did a lot of walking.

Another member of the cast was Randy Burr, R. D. 2, Evans City. Burr played the part of the sheriff. He said, "I was out in my truck when I saw some people filming at the farmhouse. When I stopped to investigate, I saw a woman with her right eye hanging out of her head running toward me." Burr said

ones in Evans City. Doak said, "They (Latent Image Inc.) started out as a firm that wanted to produce only horror movies for drive-ins. Now, they have achieved much better quality and have a bright future ahead of them."

At present, the two firms, now one, are in the process of signing the final contracts with a major film company. The film will start playing at various theatres sometime in August.

Well, anyway, the two "ghouls" who had swiped Sheriff Suck's beer were going to be scared out of their wits shortly, by seeing the "spherical luminous object" mentioned earlier come down and land in the graveyard. The teenagers from outer space were going to disembark with their pet, The Mess.

The main reason this project got scrapped was that we couldn't afford the props and special effects that would have been required to pull off the spaceship landing, The Mess, etc. We had to scale our thinking down a little in terms of logistics.

Thoughts of ghouls and burial grounds were still floating around in my sub-conscious, I guess, groping for a way to be used, because next I came up with a scenario that went like this:

A young boy runs away from home after a jealous fight with his younger brother. He is feeling rejected and unloved because his parents (or stepparents) have sided with his brother and punished him unjustly. With a few hastily packed belongings and items of food, he takes off through the woods all by himself on a cold, foggy morning. He comes into a clearing and is looking all around, hearing strange sounds and thinking he is being pursued, when suddenly there is a loud *crack*!—and he has stepped through a large pane of glass set into the ground. CLOSE-UP of his slashed ankle. Then a CLOSE-UP of his terrified face as he screams, looking downward. What he sees is that there is a rotting corpse lying flat on its back under the large pane of glass set into the earth. The boy loses consciousness and falls, blood streaming from his ankle.

The idea I had, which I told George Romero, was that in this meadow where the boy had his "accident" there would be rows of rotting corpses lying under panes of glass, like vegetables planted in a winter "hot-house" garden. Ghoulish people or alien creatures would be feeding off the human corpses, setting them under the panes of glass so that the flesh would rapidly and properly decompose to suit the ghouls' tastes.

In the first month or so after the incorporation of Image Ten, while George and I were beating around these kinds of ideas, neither of us managed to get much writing done, due to the pressures of the commercial film business. Then we got a lull...I forget why...and I didn't see George for a few days...so maybe it was some kind of long weekend. Anyway, he amazed me by coming back with about forty really excellent pages of an exciting, suspenseful story. Everybody in our group loved it. We all decided this had to

be *it*—the movie we would make. It was the first half of NIGHT OF THE LIVING DEAD. As I said, it didn't have that title yet; we were still calling it the Monster Flick. But now it was *alive*. We had something we could work with. Something that would excite and rally all our friends, associates and potential investors.

George's story used live people and ghouls and it opened in a cemetery. But it was a horror drama, not a comedy. And, instead of live

John Russo filming an up-angle shot

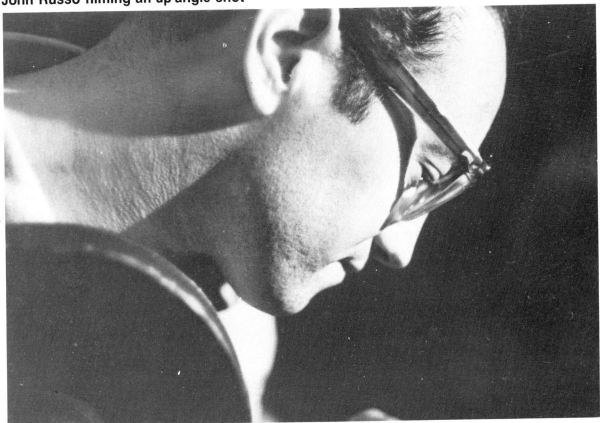

Johnny dies in the cemetery

people eating the dead, as I had suggested in my scenario about the boy running away from home, George had the dead cannibalizing the living. It clicked. It turned us all on. Because it had tension, action and horror with a small cast, not counting extras, and within logistical constraints that could be kept within our ridiculously small budget.

There are probably few people who would buy this book without having seen NIGHT OF THE LIVING DEAD. So most of you are probably familiar with the story. However, to refresh your memories, and to give you a peek at something you may not have seen before, here is the synopsis of our movie that appeared in the very first promotional booklet put out by Image Ten, Inc., and also appeared in the first press books designed by The Walter Reade Organization when they launched the picture into worldwide distribution.

SYNOPSIS
'NIGHT OF THE LIVING DEAD'
(Not For Publication)

The story opens at dusk. Barbara and her brother, Johnny, drive into the Willard cemetery to place a wreath on their father's grave. A rumpled stranger approaches and with no provocation, attacks them. Leaving Johnny lying unconscious, Barbara flees in terror to a nearby farmhouse with her attacker following behind.

Searching the house, she finds its only inhabitant; a mutilated corpse.

Barbara's bewilderment and panic reach a crescendo when she discovers her attacker is outside the house and has been joined by several other ghostly figures. It is then that Ben, a young salesman also looking for refuge from attackers, fights his way into the house and saves Barbara from the first organized siege of killers.

While boarding up the doors and windows in an attempt to keep out the increasing number of attackers, Ben explains as much of the mystery as he has learned on a news broadcast; because of a freak molecular mutation due to man's atomic research, the dead have risen to devour the living.

In the following shock sequence, Ben and Barbara discover they are not the only fugitives in the house. Judy and Tom, a teenage couple; and Helen, Harry, and their daughter Karen, have been hiding in the basement.

It is between Ben and the querulous Harry that the internal friction develops; the disagreement over where to hide and how to defend themselves with the one available weapon.

The need for help increases when a news broadcast warns that injury from a "ghoul" can infect a healthy person with the same flesh-eating "disease." The child, Karen, has been injured by one of the ghouls in her flight to the house.

Tension in the house reaches a febrile pitch as hordes of ghouls pound on the house...an escape is attempted by Tom and Judy...it fails and they are devoured.

The attackers grow stronger as the bond among the remaining survivors weakens; the doors burst open and the flesh eaters reign.

Ben accidentally shoots Harry, Barbara is dragged outside by her brother who has become a ghoul, Helen is devoured by her infected child, and only Ben survives, barricaded in the basement.

The next scene is dawn. Humanity has triumphed. Organization of the living has suppressed the organization of the dead.

A posse of farmers, police and dogs, has surrounded the farm house and is burning the last of the ghouls.

Ben, still hiding in the basement, hears help outside. Bursting out of the house wild-eyed and mute with the terror of the night, he is mistaken as one of the flesh eaters.

In one last terrible irony, Ben dies at the hands of his saviors.

62 • MAY 7, 1971

Rex Reed
Newest Splurge of Bone-Chillers Is Gravely Dug by Horror Fans

If it's true that troubled art is born out of troubled times, no wonder the movies are preoccupied with blood and viscera. And no wonder horror films are enjoying a popular revival. I've always loved them; sometimes I set my alarm clock for 3 a.m. just to watch the creeping terror. They'r... Strikes Back or Werewolf of London. They'r... ...turn up the electric blanket to... ...horror is a

The Miami Herald
Sunday
January 12, 1969

Horror Movie Matinee

Ghouls Feast On Humans as Children Weep

The traditional horror movies have been largely overlooked as the controversy rages over violence on the screen. ...cago film critic Roger Ebert ...ed a kiddie matinee to see Night of the Li...

33

Now, the way that the script got finished was that after George Romero had written the first half, a group of us—basically George, Russ Streiner, Karl Hardman, Marilyn Eastman and myself—had several meetings during which ideas were bashed around for the second half of the story. Then, with everybody's contributions in mind, I wrote the screenplay, to some extent rewriting George's half, which had been in short story form instead of screenplay format, and had gone as far as the point at which Harry and Tom come up from the basement.

In this draft, which remained the working script all through production, the male lead, Ben, was a crude, uneducated, but intelligent and resourceful truckdriver. In shooting, we had to change his character, lines and deliveries when we cast Duane Jones, an intelligent, refined young man, whose power was tempered by subtlety and restraint.

There were several other key changes made as we went along. Originally, the character Tom was the middle-aged caretaker of the

Willard Cemetery; he did not have a girl-friend. But we cast Keith Wayne in the part, a much younger man, and wrote in a girlfriend for him named Judy, so that there would be an empathetical young couple to get blown up and devoured during the escape attempt. One

A recent shot of Marilyn Eastman

Helen Cooper in the Final Siege of Ghouls

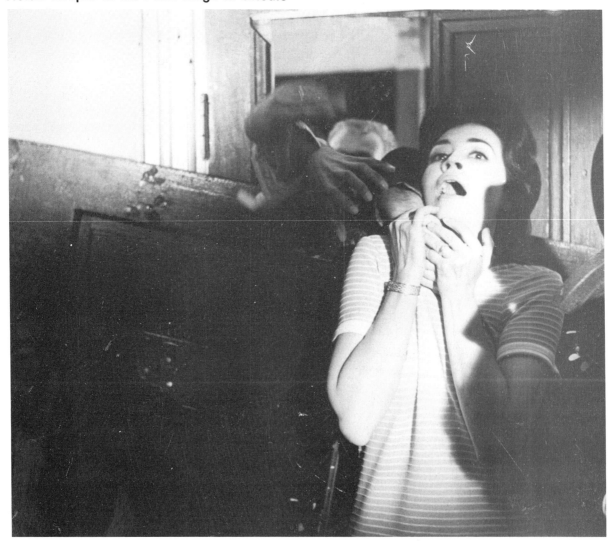

reason we took this step was that, in casting sessions, we liked the qualities that Judith Ridley exhibited and wanted to make room for her in the movie. She was very pretty and had a personal charm that came across on screen.

Also, the scenes in Washington, D.C.—the army general, the government officials, the news reporters, etc.—were inserted as an afterthought. Although our story basically dealt with a microcosm—what was happening to a small group of people in the ghoul crisis—we wanted to create the impression that it was a nationwide phenomenon, and were deeply concerned about finding ways to pull off this illusion on our inadequate budget. Things like going to Washington, D.C., plus making use of TV and radio ambiance, helped our cause and made our concept succeed.

We debated among ourselves whether or not the ghoul phenomenon needed an explanation. I didn't think it did; I thought we could simply show scientists and authority figures arguing, scrambling and struggling to get at the cause of it and find a solution—the way they would be doing in real life...and our movie would end with them still struggling. But, others in our group thought we needed an "explanation" of some sort, because science fiction and horror films up to that time had always had one. So we ended up going with the idea of the Venus probe—but we never said that it *definitely* was the cause of the "ghoul disease"—it was merely suspected.

A third major change we made in the script during shooting—and perhaps the one with the greatest impact—was to have *all* the people in the house get killed. In the working script, Barbara survives. She gets dragged down into the basement with Ben, instead of getting dragged outside by her dead brother Johnny. She's still down there when Ben goes upstairs and is accidentally shot and killed by posse members. Here is an excerpt, the last two pages of the working script, which will show you the ending that was originally written:

...a shot rings out. Ben reels, driven back, a circle of blood on his forehead, right between his eyes.

Barbara's scream is heard, from downstairs. Simultaneously, Sheriff McClelland shouts, his face flushed with anger.

McCLELLAND: Damn it, what'd you shoot for? I told you to be careful...there might be people in there...

POSSE MAN: Naw, this place is demolished, there ain't nobody in there.

PATROLMAN: I'm sure I heard a girl's scream—from the basement, maybe...

Several men have advanced to kick in the front door. They step back and peer cautiously inside. Their faces search the room. A patch of sunlight from the open door falls partially on Ben. He is dead. The men look down at him, but step past him toward the cellar. They do not know he was a man; to them he is just another dead ghoul. Then, from the cellar, they hear muffled sobs. McClelland enters and begins to inch his way down the stairs.

McCLELLAND: (shouts) Anybody down there?

He draws his pistol, inches his way down the stairs. At the bottom, he confronts Barbara, sitting wide-eyed in a chair. McClelland raises his pistol, aims it for her head. But something stops him...a tear in her eye. He lowers his weapon. The tear trickles down Barbara's cheek.

McCLELLAND: It's all right, men! Come on down! It's just a girl down here!

He goes to Barbara, bends over her, looks at her, begins to help her up.
DISSOLVE TO closing scenes. Burning of bodies in the yard of the old house. Perhaps the burning of the house itself. In the background, against a scene of McClelland draping his jacket around Barbara and bringing coffee to her lips, we see Ben's body on a stretcher, carried by two men...they lift it into the rear of the station wagon.

McCLELLAND: It's too bad...an accident...the only one we had, the whole night.
CLOSING CREDITS ROLL.

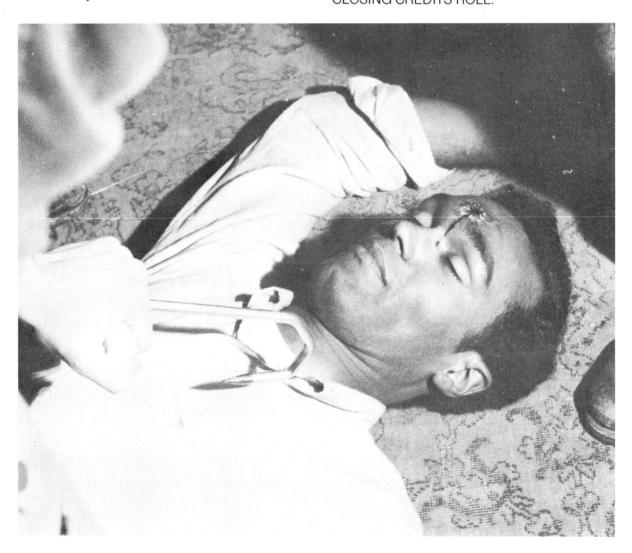

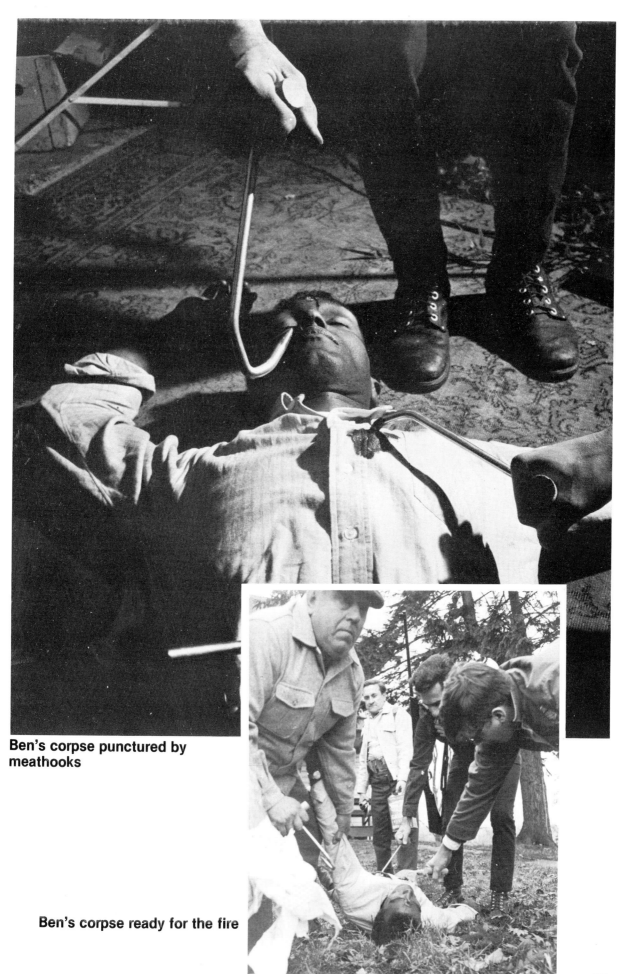

Ben's corpse punctured by meathooks

Ben's corpse ready for the fire

We had argued back and forth whether or not to kill Ben, but finally everybody agreed it was the thing to do. We figured it would shock people and they would hate it, but it would make them keep talking about the picture as they were leaving the theater. Also, after all, it is exactly the sort of thing that probably *would* happen. You couldn't have huge posses of armed and untrained men combing the countryside in a time of dire emergency without some pretty horrible accidents happening while they were all under a strain. Look what happens during deer hunting season.

We thought the redeeming factor would be if Barbara got saved. but then it was just such perfect irony that her dead brother return for her. So we went with that.

Karl Hardman suggested a third possibility that would have made an interesting ending, but it never got used. He wanted to see the little girl who devoured her parents (Harry and Helen Cooper, played by Karl Hardman and Marilyn Eastman) be standing in the foreground as the posse members finished burning the dead bodies and drove off. There would thus be one ghoul still left alive.

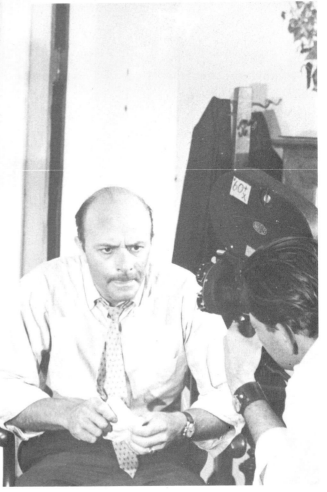

George filming Karl and Marilyn

When I finished writing the working script, it didn't even have a title on it, not even Monster Flick. It wasn't Xeroxed but was run off on an old mimeograph machine, because one of our investors had access to one and could save us money that way. The important thing was that we all liked the script and truly believed it could make a good movie. There weren't any naysayers, none of the kinds of conceptual disagreements that breed dissension and wreck a project before it can gather momentum.

Back when we were hashing out ideas, trying to come up with something, I had said to everybody, ''Whatever the *terror* is in our movie, it's got to be believable, and there has got to be plenty of it. It can't be like a typical B horror flick where you get your first peek at some aspect of a rubber monster fifteen minutes into the movie, and then you don't see it for another fifteen or twenty minutes, when it pops up and kills the town drunk. Then the scientists yack for a half hour…and in the end the army shows up with airplanes and flamethrowers, and kills the thing. Those kinds of movies never really pay off the people who pay to see them.''

The philosophy of our movie-making group was that not only did the *terror* have to be believable, but so did the people confronting it. They had to think and act the way ordinary people really would behave in a crisis.

Our working script had given us a blueprint that could satisfy these aims. We had plenty of ghouls, plenty of suspense and action. Once you accepted the premise that the dead could rise, everything that followed in our story was consistent and logical. If we didn't somehow blow it in the execution, we had an excellent shot at doing what we had set out to do, which was to really pay off the people who buy tickets to horror movies.

FEAR that deadliest of all emotions clutching at your heart·the....

NIGHT OF THE LIVING DEAD. x

Pittsburgh Post-Gazette Daily Magazine

WEDNESDAY, NOVEMBER 1, 1967

'Night of Flesh Eaters'

Pittsburghers Make Chiller For Drive-Ins

By THOMAS O'NEIL
Post-Gazette Staff Writer

OF PITTSBURGHERS has just produced a full-length movie which will be distributed nationally, but even its publicists doubt it will make this city the movie capital of

…e, a chiller-thriller designed especially for the late-late drive-in circuit, is "Night of the Flesh Eaters," co-produced by Karl Hardman. Russell W. Streiner. Hardman 's well-known to Pittsburgh radio audiences as one of the stars of the former Cordic and Co. program and the current Flake show.

…former actor and staff member at the playhouse, is vice president of Image …

★ ★ ★

…RS in the movie, all of it shot in …County, this past summer, are …ane Jones, Marilyn Eastman, …ley, and Keith Wayne.

…in the movie are Channel 11's …e, Chuck (Jason Flake) Craig, …ano, Kyra Schon, and a number of the …urgh …g members of the Pittsburgh …departments.

…cerns "flesh eaters," similar …s, who attack several victims, …royed after being trapped …house.

…rst of four such ventures …ge Ten.

Bill Heinzman portrays the first of the "flesh eaters" in the locally-produced film which will be distributed nationally this spring on the drive-in circuit.

Preparing to record one of the scenes on location in Evans City are soundmen Marshall Booth and, right, Gary Streiner.

These are some of the "victims" of the flesh eaters as depicted in a scene from the soon-to-be-released feature film.

PREPRODUCTION PITFALLS: THE MONSTER FLICK ALMOST DIES

"NIGHT OF THE LIVING DEAD remains a special film for all horror fans. It turned around our sense of terror, touching something much deeper than the usual 'bug-eyed monster' fare of drive-ins in the '50s and '60s. Like INVASION OF THE BODY SNATCHERS, NIGHT OF THE LIVING DEAD had more to say than 'Boo!'"

—Paul D. Adomites, Questar

As a kid, I had gone to see just about every one of the types of horror movies from the '50s and '60s that Paul D. Adomites was referring to in the above quote. As I mentioned in the preceding chapter, one of our main aims with our Monster Flick was to avoid making one of those trite, insipid kinds of B movies. It is very gratifying when critics and fans, like Mr. Adomites, recognize and acknowledge the extent to which we succeeded.

Some people suppose that we went into the project blind, without even so much as a written script, and got lucky. Nothing could be farther from the truth. We had some good luck along the way, but the luck was able to work to our advantage because we had formulated a project with firm structure and purpose. And within that structure we were game enough to add new and exciting wrinkles—like writing in a part for Judith Ridley, altering the depiction of the male lead so we could cast Duane Jones, letting Johnny come back and "get" Barbara, and even using the animal parts brought out to the location by one of our investors who owned a meatpacking plant. We were out to give our picture every possible chance to attract attention, to defy convention, and sell tickets.

We had the zest and determination to work together as a group to pull our ideas off. We could not have anticipated that the Monster Flick would eventually be called a "classic." But we fully expected, every step of the way, that we would make a very good motion picture of its type, better than most other pictures in the genre. We were that cocky.

One of the reasons we weren't shy about bucking the mainstream was that we couldn't be sure we'd be able to sell our product to a distributor. At that time, none of us had any experience in movie distribution. We had no contacts. It seemed that, as a court of last resort, we might have to rent screens in the Pittsburgh area and self-distribute the Monster Flick, if no national distributor would take it. We used to tell ourselves that even if this happened, we ought to be able to recoup our investment by getting the picture into local drive-ins. We even tried to ensure "word of mouth" among local moviegoers by putting the names of real towns on screen as "Rescue Centers" where survivors of ghoul attacks might go to receive treatment and protection.

In making the picture, we didn't do many things that were not carefully calculated. But in the beginning, so much planning and introspection was transpiring, and so little action was taking place, that the entire project almost died.

One of the problems was that, the script having been written, we found ourselves in the midst of a bitterly cold, late winter...far too cold to be out filming. George Romero and I went out one weekend with a camera to see what it would be like, and not only did *we* freeze, but the camera motor froze, too, and the gears stopped turning. It must've been an unusually bitter winter that year. There are camera barnies that contain little heaters; they resemble cigarette lighters and burn lighter fluid; but barnies are very cumbersome to use. And how could actors and extras be made up for outdoor scenes in zero degree weather? We certainly couldn't afford heated trailers for our "stars" like the ones major studios set up on remote locations. The project had enough impediments, on its ultra-low budget, and couldn't stand weather handicaps. The only logical thing to do was wait till spring to start shooting, even though

George and I were chomping at the bit, afraid something would happen to make the dream evaporate if we stood still for too long. But, till it warmed up outside, at least we could cast, build sets, scout locations, etc.

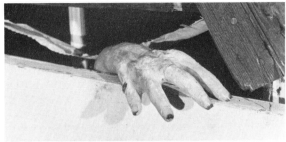

The critical location that we absolutely needed was the old farmhouse. It had to be a *real*, lived-in house. Easy enough. Sure. But we had to be able to utterly destroy it. Who was going to let us do that? Our shareholders were zealous, but not insane. Not wealthy, either. We didn't know anybody who would lend us a thirty- or forty-thousand-dollar home so we could fill it with "ghouls" and "desperate people" who would bash it to bits when we yelled, "Action!" There was no way to fake the destruction. Real windows had to be broken. Real furniture smashed up. Real nails pounded into walls, window frames and door jambs. Real fires had to be set on the porch and all over the lawn. Not exactly what your Aunt Mathilda has in mind for her tulip garden.

We couldn't afford to buy or build a house to destroy, since all the hard cash we had in our till added up to $12,000 and it had to cover all the costs of production. NOTE: The $12,000 had been put up by the first twenty investors, including ourselves. After that, as the picture neared completion, we sold more stock at a higher price per share. And Hardman Associates, Inc., and The Latent Image, Inc., extended their lines of credit with labs, art houses and other suppliers, for the total out-of-pocket cash of $60,000.

All of us went out looking in the suburbs of Pittsburgh for old houses that might have been abandoned because of construction projects. We went further out into the countryside, still looking. All we found were places so utterly decrepit, rotted and vandalized that they could never be "fixed up" to appear lived-in, not for any affordable amount of money. And if the house didn't look believable, we didn't have a movie. We could pull everything else off but that. It was the one expensive element in a script otherwise perfectly tailored within our means.

We kept working on other aspects of pre-production, while we hoped to somehow come up with a suitable farmhouse. We purchased twenty-five used, beat-up mannequins from a local company that specialized in repairing them and reselling them to clothing stores. We also bought boxes of ping-pong balls, a supply of black crepe, and a hundred pounds of modeling clay. Weird items, right? But we needed them because George, who as I said was an excellent sculptor, was going to show us how to make the mannequins into "ghouls." With the clay, we'd sculpt ghoulish features onto the faces of the mannequins. We'd use slices of ping-pong balls to give them realistic-looking white eyeballs, and we'd paint on the irises. We used the crepe to give them hair. With suitable make-up and false teeth made of plastic, they became "ghoul dummies" to be placed into the backgrounds of certain scenes or to take blows, stabs, flames and gunshots. Almost all of these "fake" ghouls ended up in our movie. (The few that didn't get destroyed were left standing in the broken, boarded-up windows of the "monster house" after we were done filming, which created a real "haunted house" and quite a conversation piece for the rural neighborhood.)

While we made props, dummies, etc., we were trying to complete the cast. There was quite a bit of hassle over this, and some internal disagreement. But some of the casting was pretty easy. We knew right away that Karl Hardman and Marilyn Eastman would play Harry and Helen Cooper, and Karl's daughter Kyra would play the Coopers' little girl, Karen, which represented a minor script change since originally the Coopers were to have a little boy instead, named Timmy. We talked Russ Streiner into playing Johnny; he was a graduate of the Pittsburgh Playhouse School of the Theater and had acted in a number of stage productions there and elsewhere. And Richard Ricci and I knew Keith Wayne, a young nightclub singer and actor, whom we suggested for the part of Tom.

George Kosana, a friend of mine from Clairton who had become an investor in Image Ten, was cast as Sheriff McClelland, even though he had no dramatic training. But we had used him in some tourist development films for the state of Pennsylvania, and knew that he had a forceful personality and a natural believability in front of the camera. He was also an extremely hard worker, all through the production. He crewed, built props, supervised the use of firearms, and performed countless other functions that were invaluable, besides acting.

Casting Judy O'Dea as Barbara was Karl and Marilyn's idea, and a very good one as it turned out. Judy had been born in Pittsburgh, had enjoyed wide acclaim in stage presentations all over the United States, and was pursuing her career in Hollywood. She came back to her hometown to do a great job in NIGHT OF THE LIVING DEAD.

For a long time we had no one we really liked as Ben. We thought that Rudy Ricci, who happened to be an excellent actor as well as a writer, might do the part, but Rudy was busily working on a novel and didn't really want to act in the Monster Flick unless it became absolutely necessary. Actually, he seemed to have a disdain for the project; his novel meant a lot more to him, to the point where I had to coax him for three weeks to kick in his six hundred dollars and become one of the ten original investors. I used to tell him, "You think your novel is the most important thing in your life right now, but you're going to be surprised when this little horror film is the thing that really does it for us all." Accurate and prophetic words, if I do say so myself.

A friend of ours, Betty Ellen Haughey, gave us the suggestion of casting Duane Jones as Ben. George Romero, Betty Ellen, and some others of our group had known Duane from a few years back, when he had been living in Pittsburgh. But he had gone to New York to study at the Actors Studio. He came back to audition, and we were highly impressed. He was stunned when he got the role, and told us he had assumed we would give the edge to Rudy Ricci, since Rudy was an insider and an investor as well. But we had all voted for Duane, even Rudy.

At about this time, through a stroke of luck, we found the farmhouse we needed as the primary location. This came about because we had taken on, as an apprentice, an art-school student named Jack Ligo. When Jack happened to overhear the details of what we were looking for, he mentioned a possibility: a large white farmhouse in Evans City that was going to be bulldozed to the ground because the owners were intending to use the property as a sod farm. We hightailed it out to look at the place, about forty miles north of Pittsburgh, and it looked perfect. After some negotiations, the owner agreed to rent it to us for several months for about $300 per month, and then bulldoze it. It had last seen use as a summer camp for a church group. It had no running water, and while we were working there we had to carry our water from a spring down a steep hill, quite a distance away. The house didn't have a suitable basement for filming, either; the beams were too low, and the floor was mud. So we decided to film our basement scenes on a set built in the basement of the building where The Latent Image was headquartered.

By the time all these arrangements were made, it was already spring. The weeks were flying by. No actual shooting date had been set. And some lethargy and vacillation was

Duane Jones relaxing between takes

setting in. For some reason, the casting decisions, the choice of the Evans City farmhouse, and some other key points were being second-guessed. I am a pretty direct, straightforward person once I get moving on something, and the delays upset me. I figured that from past experience everybody ought to realize how easily projects could fall apart, so we had to keep taking steps to make sure that did not happen.

Already, during the winter, the production had almost taken a turn which to me, at the time, was pretty strange and threatening. At a meeting between George, Russ, Karl, Marilyn and myself, George had offered the directorship to Karl Hardman. Karl had hesitated in accepting, and I had leapt into the breech, saying, ''Well, if neither of you two guys wants to do it, *I'll* direct.'' I had said this only to confuse the issue and prevent any final decision from being made right at that moment.

A recent shot of Karl Hardman

Hardman Associates was into radio production more than film production, and I had never seen Karl work in any capacity other than actor; neither had most of the people in Latent Image's camp. We weren't so much voting against Karl, but *for* George. Maybe the movie would've been successful with Karl instead of George as director, but it is virtually certain that it would've been a quite *different* movie because of the differing styles and priorities of the two personalities. To me, being willing to give up the directorship so easily was an example of George's natural modesty and generosity, and his failure to realize how much of a leader he was.

George wearily studying the next camera placement

As George, Russ and I walked up Fort Pitt Boulevard to The Latent Image after the meeting, I said, ''I really don't want to direct, George, I want you to direct, but if I hadn't said anything you would've given it to Hardman. Everybody in our group wants you, and if you're not director they'll lose interest in the project. You've been our main guy all these years, and it's going to be silly and maybe disastrous if you don't take the reins now that we're finally going to make a feature movie—the thing we've fought for and killed ourselves for, from the beginning.''

After some more pep-talking and discussing, we agreed to get firmly behind George Romero as director—something that I had never previously thought was even at issue. As far as I know, Karl Hardman might have made an excellent director. But at that time

NIGHT OF THE LIVING DEAD

SUCCESS
Horror film no nightmare for Pittsburgh movie men

RARE GOOD SHOCKER

Gem of a horror film possesses all the earmarks of a ''sleeper.'' Strong stuff for delicate stomachs.

44

One of the main reasons for the stalling of the project in the spring, besides the vacillation I mentioned earlier, was that commercial filmmaking is a seasonal business, and with the good shooting weather we started to be hit with quite a few ad-agency jobs. We needed them to pay the rent, but if we couldn't find a way to sandwich in some work on the Monster Flick, the summer would dribble away, and we wouldn't have a feature film in the can. More and more, it was beginning to look as though that was going to happen, and I grew increasingly disgruntled. So did George. One day at The Latent Image, I fell to really bitching about the lack of progress and telling everybody that things were doomed to fall apart if we didn't go full speed ahead and damn the consequences.

George, who was completely swamped with some commercial gigs for which the clients had demanded only him as their cinematographer and editor, told me that I should take over as production manager and simply do whatever needed to be done to keep the project moving. "I'll be glad to," I said,

"but only under one condition: that I have full and absolute authority. Because I'm going to have to maybe step on some people's toes to end all the indecision."

"Fine with me," said George.

"All right," I enthused. "As of today, all of the cast and locations will be finalized, and we're going to start getting ready to film in Evans City."

I made a raft of phone calls informing everybody concerned about the final decisions and mustering their support. It was during late April and early May that the big push got underway. Right then, Gary Streiner, Vince Survinski and I weren't as tied up as George Romero and Russ Streiner, so we concentrated on outfitting the house in Evans City. It had to be thoroughly cleaned and refurbished—filled with rugs, furniture, appliances and knickknacks. We rented a U-Haul truck and bought a truckload of furnishings from a Goodwill store for fifty dollars. Additional stuff was contributed by shareholders.

Karl & Duane rehearsing with Keith Wayne

45

George Kosana procured the big-game trophies that dressed up the study and scared Barbara when she came sneaking in there. He had personally shot the wild boar on one of his various hunting expeditions during vacations from his job in a steel mill. He also supplied the lever-action Winchester rifle that Ben uses in the movie.

Vince Survinski built a workable fireplace where there had been none, taking out part of a wall and laying bricks and a hearth. The script called for a fireplace so Ben could light the torches he used to battle the ghouls. Vince also rigged the cellar door so it could be barricaded. But first he had to put a make-believe cellar door in one of the walls. The actors would be seen going through it, but when they went down the stairs we would be cutting to the basement of the building on Fort Pitt Boulevard where The Latent Image had its offices—and people watching the movie wouldn't know the difference.

By the time we finished pitching in, the "Monster House" looked lived-in and it was set up according to screenplay requirements. Now we were ready to move cast and crew out there and actually start making our movie.

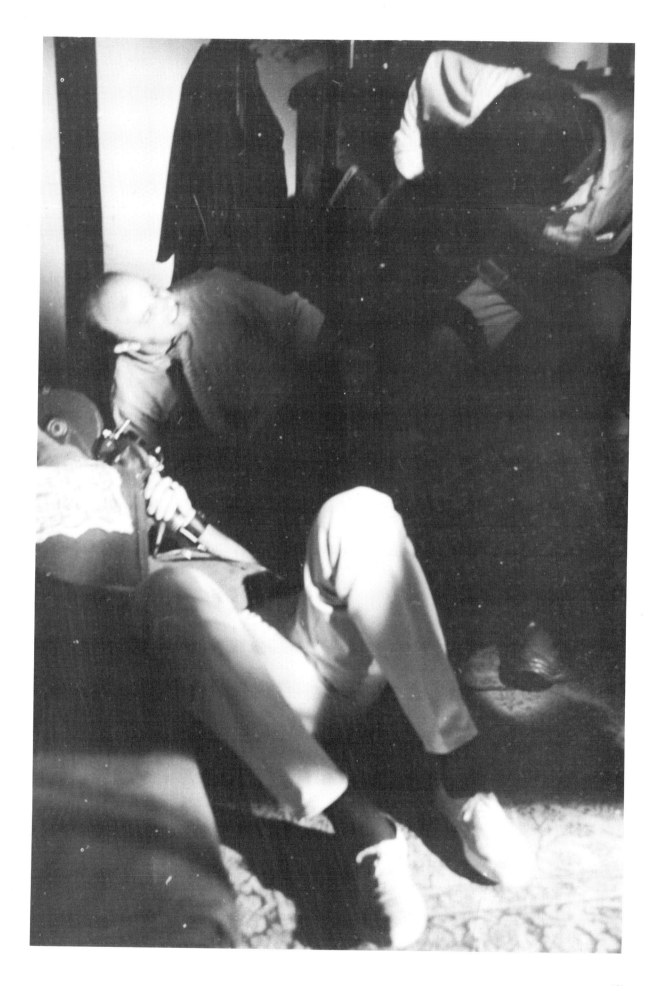

BUDGETARY RESTRICTIONS: HOW THEY AFFECTED THE MONSTER FLICK

"NIGHT OF THE LIVING DEAD, a low-budget, black-and-white film made in the Pittsburgh area...is one of the best horror films since Don Siegal's INVASION OF THE BODY SNATCHERS. The fact that the uniformly good cast is completely unknown enhances the movie's basic air of authenticity, and throughout there is the feeling that these are real people fighting the nightmarish horror threatening to engulf them. An uncommonly good shocker."

—Peter Harris, Toronto Daily Star

From the outset, we knew there were certain handicaps that we could not overcome with ingenuity. We had to live with them and attempt, as much as possible, to turn them into pluses instead of minuses.

We couldn't afford to film in 35-millimeter color. We could have used 16-millimeter and blown it to 35, but we were leery about how good the blow-up might look. It might have turned out too grainy and contrasty, as blow-up techniques at that time weren't as sophisticated as they are now. And we weren't sure we could sell our picture to a distributor if we had to walk in with a blow-up.

So we decided to go with 35-millimeter black-and-white. There were still a few major pictures being made in that format in the late '60s. One was IN COLD BLOOD. But most pictures were being made in color and in Cinemascope to compete with the little black-and-white TV screens that were in most people's homes.

One advantage of shooting in black-and-white was that our make-ups and effects didn't have to be sweated so much. For instance, sometimes we used red ink for blood, and other times we used chocolate syrup, depending on whether we wanted it to streak or splatter. Either substance was dark enough to register well for the camera.

I'd like to defend our movie in one particular: it was *not* "a grainy little movie" as it had been called by at least one reviewer. It was shot with the same types of lenses, camera and filmstock as were used on most Hollywood productions. The first prints, pulled by WRS Motion Picture Laboratory in Pittsburgh, were of superb quality and would stack up against any major studio release. But later, to save money, and without consulting us, our distributor had a number of prints pulled on a cheap, inferior stock. These are the prints that were criticized and caused our professionalism to be questioned. Even today, there are a number of pirated prints in circulation that don't do the picture justice.

The camera we used, although of excellent quality, was a liability compared to today's lightweight, easily portable lip-synch cameras. Modern cameras are self-blimped and extremely silent. The one we used, because we were able to purchase it cheaply, was a 35-millimeter Arriflex housed inside a huge, eighty-pound blimp, whose function was to seal in the sound of the camera's grinding gears so the actors' voices would be in the clear. Naturally, this cumbersome apparatus wasn't very maneuverable. It restricted the angles and the kinds of shots we were able to frame, except when we weren't shooting lip-synch and could use the camera without the blimp. And, of course, it slowed us down as we attempted to move from one set-up to another and get the maximum out of each shooting day. It affected the choice of sets and locations, as we had to have large rooms and ample working space for the bulky blimp and all the other necessary gear.

We couldn't afford cranes, dollies, booms, sound stages, and many other niceties that are taken for granted on major productions and which enhance any movie's overall look. We *were* able to work in some helicopter shots when the chopper owned by KQV, a local radio station, showed up to cover us for a news report and the pilot was nice enough to help us out, above and beyond the call of duty. We were constantly on the look-out for "frills" like this that we could incorporate to make our production look not-so-low-

48

Bill Hinzman & George Romero on a camera set-up

A big set-up during Posse Day

budget.

We were worried that we did not have enough money to pay a sufficient number of extras. But we got plenty of volunteers, including people from in and around Evans City, who jumped at the chance to be in a movie. We let them be posse members or made them up as ghouls. They were patient and enthusiastic. They gave the movie a "real people" look that probably added to the believability.

We couldn't afford a make-up specialist either. Some of the actors did their own, including all of the principles. Karl Hardman and Marilyn Eastman made up most of the ghouls. Karl and Marilyn really carried quite a load, because they also took most of the production stills *and* developed and printed them in vast quantities for our publicity campaign. This is in addition to acting key roles and performing numerous other functions.

We hired Joe Unitas as a lighting technician, on a per diem basis, because Joe didn't want to work for a percentage of the picture's profits. For trivia fans: Joe Unitas happens to be a cousin of Johnny Unitas, the famous Baltimore Colt quarterback. He would've made a lot more money if he would have taken the percentage we offered him.

Vince Survinski's brother Regis, who was one of our investors, fortunately for us was a fireworks and demolitions expert. We would have been hard-pressed to pay for that specialty, and we really needed it. Rege and his partner, Tony Pantanello, did all of our explosive effects—gunshot squibs, truck blowing up, etc. They also made blank ammunition. And they acted as posse members, ghouls, and so forth, in various changes of make-up and costume.

Of course we could not afford to buy and process ample filmstock. The Monster Flick was shot on a ratio of six-to-one; that is, we shot only six times as much footage as ended up in the finished edit. Most Hollywood pictures are shot on a ratio of about twenty-five to-one, so that every possible angle is covered and there are plenty of safety takes. There came a point about halfway through our shooting schedule when George Romero was just winging it—getting only two or even *one* good take and then going on to the next shot—and if he had missed anything critical, we would have been hit hard, especially if we had found out we needed something at the Monster House after it had been bulldozed to the ground. But George did what he had to do, out of necessity.

Marilyn Eastman doubling as a ghoul

Since we couldn't pay security guards to stand watch over our gear, part of the crew had to live at the house during filming. The ones who did this were George, Gary, Vince and I. We slept on canvas cots bought from an army surplus store. We carried our own water from the far-away spring, and we boiled it on a hot-plate to take cat baths.

George is 6'4'' tall and his cot was too short for him. His feet stuck out over the edge. Every night before lying down on it he'd say, matter-of-factly, ''This thing will never hold me.'' I always wondered why he would say that. Till one night when he said it, went to lie down, and with a loud rip fell through to the floor, which became his bed from then on.

There were so many useful things we couldn't afford, it was ridiculous. Most so-called ''low-budget movies'' aren't nearly *so* low-budget or so ambitious in scope. Our big advantage was that we had no shortage of talent, ability and ''sweat equity.'' A big piece of all of us went into that movie. By ''all of us'' I mean to include our shareholders, business associates and friends. *People* made the difference. People with drive, guts, determination and loyalty made it possible for us to pull off the phenomenon that NIGHT OF THE LIVING DEAD has become.

Staging a scene for a Channel 11 Newscast—Romero, Russo, O'Dea with Dave James

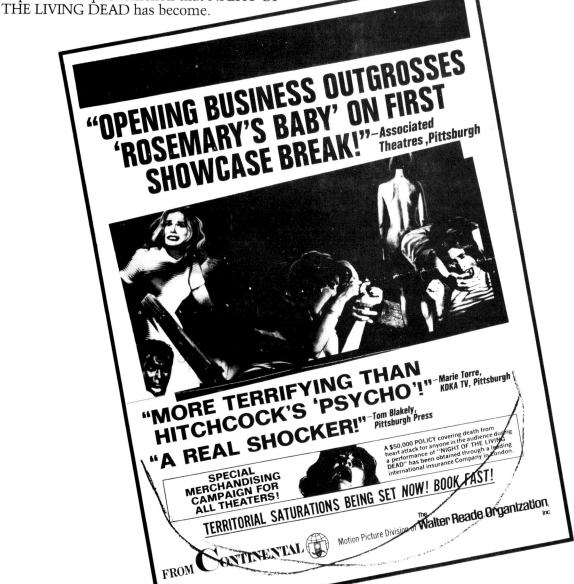

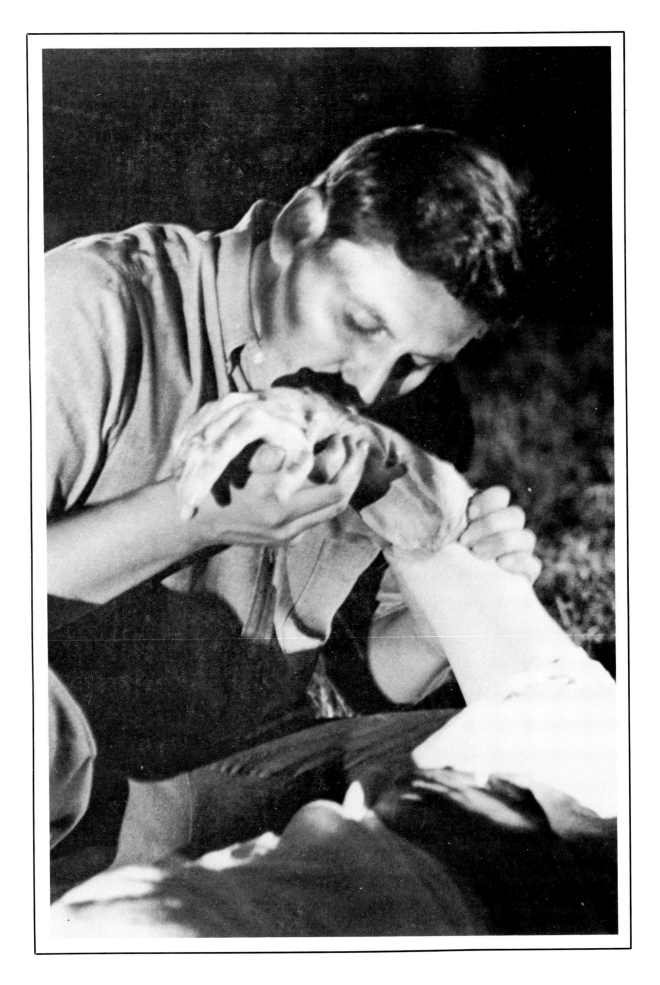

BLOW BY BLOW:
GETTING IT IN THE CAN

"You get what you pay for in NIGHT OF THE LIVING DEAD, a horror film that has the power to literally horrify. How sweet it is."
—Kenneth Turan, Washington Post

I guess just about everybody knows that movies usually are not shot in the order that the scenes appear in the script, but in the order dictated by logistical and budgetary factors. The Monster Flick certainly was no exception. In fact, our scenes had to be shot more "out of order" than most productions because actors weren't always available when we needed them; we couldn't afford to keep them in a fancy hotel close to the location for the duration of the shooting schedule. So we were always boarding up and "unboarding up" the doors and windows of the Monster House according to what moment it was supposed to be in the story. And we were always "making daylight" or "making nightfall" by covering and uncovering the doors and windows with black seamless paper. We had the boards labeled on their reverse sides so we'd remember where they belonged, for the sake of continuity. One of the things that made for long shooting days was that our story took place mostly at night. During daylight hours, we'd film in the house, using the artificial nighttime created by black seamless paper; then when the real night came, we'd do our exteriors. This usually meant that we wouldn't wrap until dawn.

For the sake of clarity, I'm going to discuss the filming of the Monster Flick in the order that the scenes appear in the finished movie. I'm going to hit the highlights, telling what I hope will be interesting anecdotes and answering the questions that seem to have intrigued fans over the years. Some scenes I may not choose to comment upon because I cannot recall anything so striking about their execution. Let them speak for themselves.

All right then, here goes:

The opening, in the cemetery. This was the last scene we filmed. We had three major bursts of shooting on the Monster Flick; the first burst was at the farmhouse because we

had to finish what we needed there so it could be bulldozed. Then we did another burst in the middle of the summer. And because of intervening stretches of commercial work we didn't get around to the cemetery stuff till late fall. In fact, the leaves were mostly off of the trees, except of course for the pine trees which we tried to shoot against. This was one of the places where shooting in black-and-white really meant something, because in color there would've been no way to disguise the fact that most of the leaves were gone and the ones that were left were gold, red, brown and yellow instead of green. Also, the actors had to try not to breathe too much while they were talking, since it was so cold we could see their white breath. What a continuity problem! Our story was supposed to have taken place within sixteen hours; we worried that it would appear to be fall one day and summer the very next morning. But it ended up working out okay.

The cemetery was in Evans City. I mention this because so many people swear they recognize it as their hometown cemetery. People from dozens of different towns.

The Animators, Inc., headed by Bob Wolcott and housed in the same building as The Latent Image, designed our opening credits and closing credits, too. Bob and some others from his company also appeared as extras in our movie.

As I mentioned, Bill Hinzman was the ghoul in the cemetery. He also was an investor. And he helped out with many other aspects of the production.

Russ Streiner's mother was also an investor, and we used her car as the car driven by Johnny and Barbara. It had been in an accident and already had a smashed fender. We made it look as though this had happened when Barbara, chased by the cemetery ghoul, crashes the car into a tree. That way we could have a "car wreck" in our movie without pay-

ing for it. We also had the ghoul smash the car window, and then paid to replace it, but this didn't cost much, and the car had to go to the body shop anyway.

We created "lightning" by flashing Color-tran lights off and on. We did it for the eerie effect, and also because there was a light drizzle while we were filming, and we were afraid it'd be noticed by the audience—and there wasn't any rain in the later story sequences we had already filmed. We reasoned, and dared to hope, that it might look like the kind of rain that dries up quickly. But it never registered on celluloid, so we lucked out.

Barbara runs from the cemetery. This was the first segment filmed. It became immediately apparent that Judy O'Dea was going to put her all into her part. She ran, fought, and did everything else required of her with the wild, high energy of someone whose life is truly in danger.

When she stumbles onto the property where the Monster House is, the first sign of human life she encounters is the outbuilding where there is a gasoline pump. We had to buy a pump and set it up there so the truck could explode when the people were trying to get gas and escape.

Barbara explores the Monster House. All the lighting here was done for eerie, ominous effect. Lots of shadows. We used "gobos"—big pieces of black seamless with weird patterns cut out, so that light can be shined through. They are a pain to constantly position and reposition and to work around. But they lent a nice texture to our movie, which people seem to appreciate. In fact, they say the picture "really worked" in black-and-white, more so than it might have in color, and I think the care taken in mood lighting is the reason why.

The corpse at the top of the stairs. George Romero made this prop out of an "educational toy" available in hobby shops, called The Living Skull. He assembled the plastic skull and "dressed it up" with false hair, skin (modeling clay), ping-pong ball eyes, and various make-up materials and paint. An excellent job! The body was that of a mannequin. People have asked us why this "dead woman" never came back to life. While making the movie, we didn't think this needed an explanation; to us, it seemed obvious that her head had been so cannibalized and destroyed that there wasn't enough of a brain left to "animate" a ghoul.

Ghouls bash out the truck headlights. We bought this truck for fifty dollars from a junk-yard so we could afford to blow it up. It was in running condition when we bought it, but then it completely died. How were Ben and Tom going to drive it to the gas pump to make the escape attempt? By sheer coincidence, a man who lived down the road from the Monster House owned exactly the same kind of truck, and it was in good running condition; he loaned it to us for the scenes where the truck had to be capable of movement. We didn't bash out the headlights. Tim Ferrante, who wrote an article on me for FANGORIA MAGAZINE, happened to notice this and asked me about it, but he's the only person who has ever mentioned it. Obviously, most people can't tell, and that's what we were betting on.

Ghoul stabbed with tire iron. This was my first appearance in the movie. I played the part because I had to stay on the location anyway, and we could give the actors a break and let them go home. Karl Hardman did my make-up. My head wound was sculpted with Dermawax, with a hole scooped out for a dollop of blood that would run when my head smacked the floor. One of the ghoul dummies that I made out of a mannequin took my place when I had to be cremated. I was not willing to go that far.

Another ghoul stabbed in the face. This was Jack Rozzo, a friend and investor. He was wearing pajamas and a bathrobe. We tried to make variations in the wounds and costumes of the flesheaters, to indicate that they must have died in the midst of different normal activities. Remember, these were supposed to be the recently dead come back to life.

56

The music box. Barbara, wandering around in shock, inadvertently turns it on. This is a chance for George to get "arty" with the hand-held camera and give the movie some "tone." These kinds of passages didn't usually occur in B horror movies. But we took the time to do them.

Ben's long speech. He had a lot to get across while he was tearing off table legs to make torches. He had to grab the audience here and make them like him. Duane Jones succeeded because he was a sensitive actor with a good screen presence—a real plus as the male lead.

Barbara's speech. Less critical than Ben's, but still very important. She did it well. We inserted a line for Judy O'Dea where she half-deliriously complains about being hot. This was so she could start unbuttoning her coat and not have to wear it under the hot movie lights all during filming. Ben finishes opening the coat after he knocks her unconscious.

The old radio. This antique was owned by Karl Hardman. Over it, we hear Civil Defense messages. The voice is that of Chuck Craig, of Hardman Associates at that time, star of a radio show that Karl produced called The Jason Flake Show. Chuck was also the studio commentator on the TV, later in the movie.

Ben lights torches, sets chairs on fire. He did this to drive away ghouls who were starting to congregate in the front yard. We show him using charcoal-lite, but actually we had to use gasoline to do the trick. During the filming of an exterior scene, where we had to start the chair in the yard smoldering again, Gary Streiner had a bad accident. He squirted gasoline on hot embers, and it went up. Gary was running in flames when Bill Hinzman tackled him, smothered the flames, and probably saved his life.

Ben finds shoes for Barbara. When he is giving the shoes to her, he tells her everything is

boarded up tight, yet the window directly behind him is not boarded. Actually, the reason we did not board it is because it was so high off the ground it was inaccessible. But it looks like a mistake, so it is one. We should've boarded it.

The first ghoul Ben shoots. Richard Ricci played this part. He gets shot twice in the chest, but he only dies when he is drilled through the head. People begin to get the idea that you have to destroy a ghoul's brain.

Back during our scripting sessions, we discussed various methods that might be appropriate and believable ways of vanquishing ghouls. Karl and Marilyn joked that maybe at the climax of the film when the ghouls swarm en masse into the house, Ben could discover that they die when they're hit in the face with a Boston cream pie. Then, at the wrap-up, a pie truck could arrive and save the day.

The nude ghoul. We used an artists' model for this scene. We figured that some of the dead bodies in morgues would have risen, and we wanted to illustrate this point. It was another "believability factor" as far as we were concerned. We also didn't mind any word-of-mouth that might accrue regarding one of the few nudes to appear in horror movies at this time.

The ghoul who eats the insect. This was Marilyn Eastman in a double role. She did her own make-up, which was quite hideous and effective.

Judy comes up from the cellar. Since this part wasn't in the original script, we made up lines and "business" for Judith Ridley as we went along, except for the scene between her and Keith Wayne, which was fully written.

The Coopers in the basement. There is a bad jump-cut in the middle of this scene. This is because the distributor *insisted* that several minutes be taken out of it, and we had no cutaway shots to use. I made the jump-cut when I was getting the negative ready to go to the lab for release prints. I attempted to match Karl's head positions as best I could. Much as I hated to do it, I figured the movie wasn't going to bomb on the basis of this one "blivet" and that has been the case.

The TV broadcasts. The television studio set was built at Hardman Associates. Chuck

Craig was the commentator. Frank Doke was very effective as Doctor Grimes, who explains about the "cadaver in the cold room." Other Hardman Associates employees helped

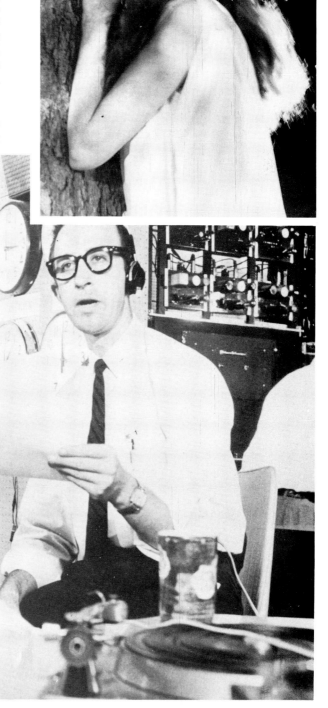

populate the studio set. This is also where we started putting the "Rescue Centers" on screen, which were really names of local towns.

The TV broadcast cuts to Washington, D.C., and George Romero does a cameo as a reporter. Another reporter is Rege Survinski. Mark Ricci, Rudy's brother, is the scientist. Al McDonald is the general; he was an advertising man whom we had worked for. Sam Solito, a local actor, plays the part of a civilian official.

I also make an appearance, in my old army uniform, as the driver of the general's staff car.

Judy and Tom's scene. George Romero wrote this at five in the morning, when he and I had had about three hours' sleep and the actors were on their way to the location. I thought it sounded pretty good when George read it to me, but maybe that was because I was so relieved that he managed to get something on paper that we could use, when my own head was drawing nothing but blanks. We needed a scene to gain empathy for the young couple just before they are blown up and devoured by ghouls. I guess it accomplishes that purpose, even if it's a bit tacky.

Molotov cocktails. This is where I got set on fire. I said to George, "*Somebody* has to catch fire in this sequence, because it won't be believable to have so many molotov cocktails bursting all around and none of the slow-moving ghouls get hit." So I volunteered. Even though everbody was worried, especially in light of what had happened to Gary Streiner, we were also thrilled to be getting the stunt on camera. It worked out fine, and we were even able to get several takes. When I felt myself getting hot, I'd fall to the ground, and people were ready with blankets to smother the flames.

The escape attempt. This was a major sequence for us since it required a large number of ghouls (extras), gunshot squibs and molotov cocktail effects, and the truck had to be blown up. Rege Survinski and Tony Pantanello were on hand to do their stuff.

When I was making phone calls to round up extras, I was stunned when at first Rudy Ricci told me he wouldn't be coming out to the location. He hadn't done anything on the film since the casting sessions when he had been a possibility for the part of Ben. When we had started production, he had gone on a vacation to Florida. I figured, all right, maybe he really needed a vacation, but now he was back and

Judy about to be blown up

he still didn't want to help us out. I told him that I could not believe that now that we were really *doing* a feature, he was going to sit on the sidelines. He ended up coming to the location. He's the ghoul who hangs onto the truck bumper as it heads for the gas pump. But it was the only night he worked on the picture. This was disappointing to me because I had imagined that if the opportunity to make any kind of feature movie ever truly materialized, *all* of our original group would pull together wholeheartedly. But, as I said, it seemed that Rudy had a disdain for the horror genre, and the novel he was writing was more important to him.

We filmed the exploding truck with three cameras in order to try and make sure we would get it. George, Russ and I were the three cameramen. We didn't know how violent the explosion was going to be. So we had the cameras placed back quite a ways, but still we almost got hit by flying shrapnel.

Ghouls feast. Many, many friends, investors and associates appeared as ghouls ''dining'' on animal organs, which were supposed to be the incinerated remains of Judy and Tom. Some of the body parts were made from parts of mannequins. For instance, the arm with blistered flesh was made from a mannequin arm coated with strands of Silly Putty. The substance looked remarkably like flesh in black-and-white, whereas in color it would've been too pink.

One of the strangest scenes I've ever come across occurred on the morning we were getting ready to shoot the ghoul feast. I walked outside of the Monster House, and there was Vince Survinski on the porch, filling Coke bottles with water and then carefully pouring the water into animal entrails. It was a weird and yet somehow a comic sight. Vince explained that when the entrails were empty they were too flat and ''lifeless'' to look squirmy enough for the camera.

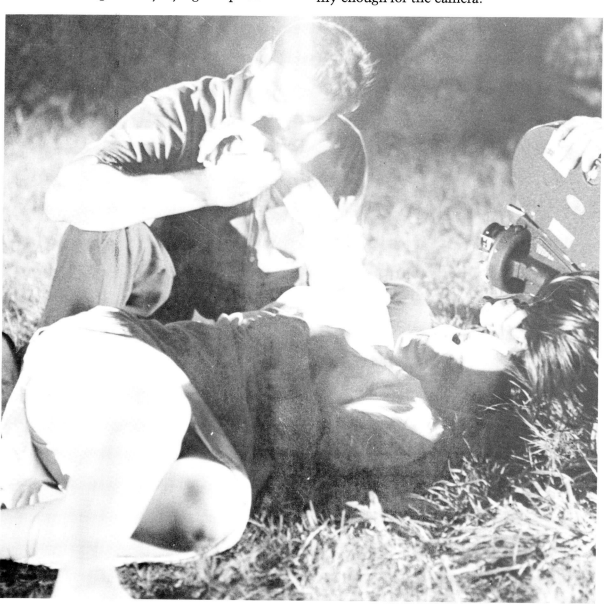

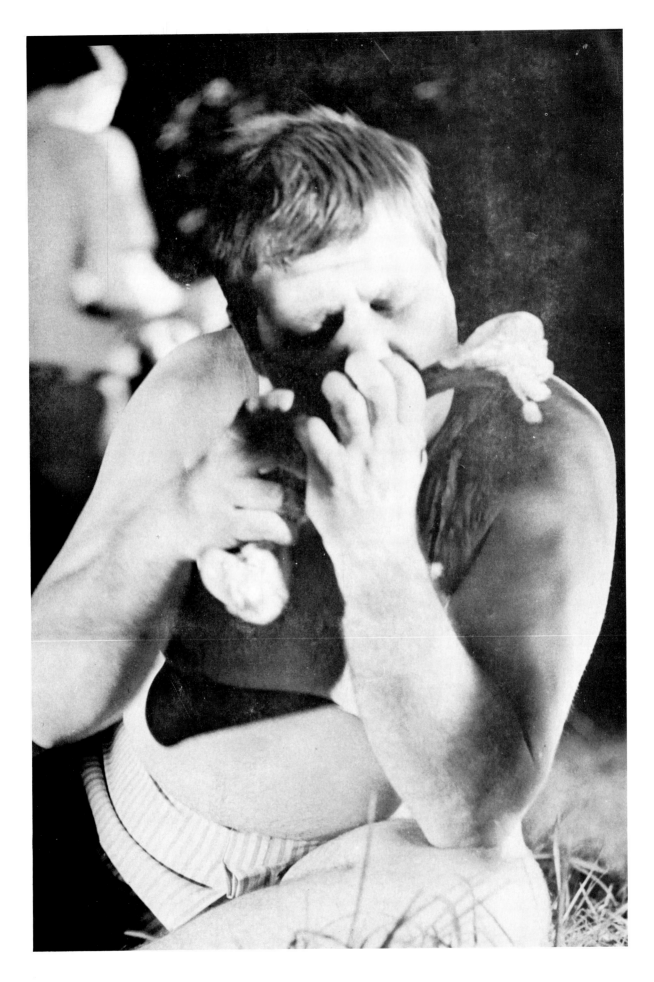

The posse on TV. "Posse Day" was another major event in the shooting schedule. We had to coordinate dozens of extras, many of whom would be toting their own firearms. Safety was a primary consideration. What if a live round got put into one of these dozens of guns, instead of a blank? We enforced a rule that anyone carrying a gun had to report to George Kosana immediately upon arrival at the location. He did a safety check on every single weapon. He and I had both been in the military, and we explained to everybody that a blank fired at close range directly at somebody could be deadly—just because it was a blank, didn't mean it was harmless.

Later in the Monster Flick, there were scenes where the sheriff and the posse appeared "live" rather than on TV, and all this stuff was shot on our big Posse Day, too. I filmed the posse activity in 16-millimeter to be matted onto the TV screen, while George Romero filmed in 35-millimeter for the sequences that weren't to appear on the TV.

We were able to drum up lots of cooperation. David Craig, the actual Safety Director of the City of Pittsburgh, came out and appeared in the film. So did four Pittsburgh policemen with their police dogs. I already mentioned the KQV helicopter. People from Channel 11 TV also helped us tremendously: Steve Hutsko, a news cameraman, and Bill "Chilly Billy" Cardille, who was host of a popular Saturday evening horror show. Bill Cardille is the TV reporter who interviews the sheriff in our movie. An interesting sidelight is that his daughter, Lori Cardille, currently has the female lead in George Romero's DAY OF THE DEAD. Channel 11 gave our picture plenty of publicity. Dave James, one of their news men, came out to the location to interview us, and he also appeared in the movie as an extra.

"Chilly Billy" Cardille interviews George Kosana

Keith Wayne on-camera

63

When we were about to film Cardille's interview with Sheriff McClelland, I told George Kosana that it wasn't important to say his lines exactly as they were written; it would come off more like a real interview if he simply had in his own mind a body of information about the ghouls, and used this body of information to respond to the interviewer's questions. As it turned out, he had his lines memorized well and used many of them verbatim. He was really a very good, natural actor. His most famous line—"They're dead, they're all messed up"—was his own invention, and we loved it.

Many of our most colorful posse members were from the town of Clairton, and were enlisted by George Kosana. Clairton is an iron-and-steel town with a special vitality, it seems. Some of its zaniness was captured in the movie, THE DEER HUNTER, which was partially filmed there. But I happen to think that the real Clairtonites are wilder and zanier than the actors in DeNiro's movie. Seven of the investors in Image Ten were from Clairton, including George Kosana and myself. They *like* being in movies, and some of them have appeared in three others that I was involved with, after NIGHT OF THE LIVING DEAD.

The final siege. While the ghouls are finally overwhelming the people in the house, Harry Cooper gets his hands on the rifle, but Ben takes it off of him and shoots him. Originally, the way I wrote this was that Ben was going to get some help from Harry's child who, having turned into a ghoul, grabs Harry from behind and drags him downstairs, enabling Ben to seize the rifle. But we decided to have Ben just wrestle the rifle away and shoot Harry. Filming this got pretty comic and frustrating because when Karl Hardman was "dying" he kept getting tangled up in the coat stand and dragging it through the doorway. We had to do a lot of takes to get the scene in the can.

The little girl, Karen, cannibalizes her mother and father. Helen Cooper's death is particularly horrible. At that time, I don't think it would have gotten an R rating; neither would many of the other scenes in NIGHT OF THE LIVING DEAD. But our eventual distributor, Continental Pictures, a division of The Walter Reade Organization, did not subscribe to the rating code.

Critic Roger Ebert wrote an article in the *Chicago Sun-Times* that lashed out at the kinds of people who would allow children to see a movie loaded with such horrid, mind-

Karen almost gets Ben

Foreign versions of the NOLD novel

DIE NACHT DER LEBENDEN TOTEN

NIGHT OF
THE LIVING DEATH

D
Sensation de
Filmfestspie
in Edinburg

Regie: George A. Rom
mit Judith O'Dea, Duane Jon
Marilyn Eastr
Eine IMAGE TEN-Produkt
der Prof

D
Gruselschocke
des Jahr

66

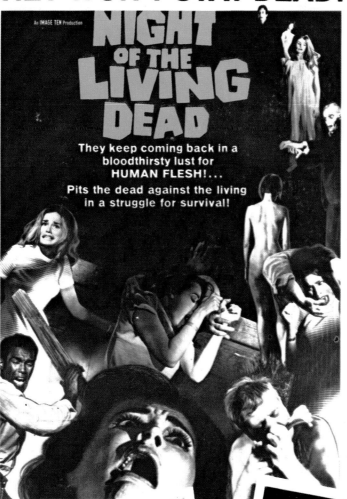

PER DIVORARE GLI ESSERI CHE VIVONO

LA NOTTE DEI MORTI VIVENTI

shattering scenes; but we had no control over this. Later, Ebert's article appeared in *The Reader's Digest*. Here is what he said: "I felt real terror in that neighborhood theater. I saw kids who had no sources they could draw upon to protect themselves from the dread and fear they felt. Censorship isn't the answer to something like this—it never is. But I would be ashamed to argue for the 'right' of those little girls and boys to see that film...what are parents thinking of when they dump their kids off to see a film titled NIGHT OF THE LIVING DEAD?"

Ghouls surrounding Ben's truck

The flesheater's overrun the farmhouse

Vince Survinski shoots Ben. Yes, good old Vince Survinski has the dubious distinction of playing the posse member who drills our "good guy" right between the eyes. Here is what Vince had to say about it, some years later, in *Questar Magazine*: "Well, I realized my childhood ambition to be a 'movie actor.' But that was squelched when I went to a kiddies' matinee to see the film. When the scene came where I shot the hero, those kids' reactions scared the hell out of me. I stayed in the theater till it was cleared, then made a hasty exit and headed for a nearby alley. I think those kids would have pelted me with half-eaten candy bars, gooey popcorn, soda pop and whatever."

I suppose I can't add anything to that except: Oh, well, Vince, such is the price of fame.

The ghoul & the good guy about to be cremated (above)   The posse takes a break (below)

BE LUCKY IF HE LIVES AS IT IS NOW."

TRUCKDRIVER: (more impersonal than ever before) "OKAY. NOW YOU'RE HIS FATHER. IF YOU'RE DUMB ENOUGH TO GO DIE IN THAT TRAP, IT'S YOUR BUSINESS. BUT I AIN'T DUMB ENOUGH TO GO WITH YOU. IT'S JUST BAD LUCK FOR THE KID THAT HIS OLD MAN'S SO DUMB...NOW GET THE HELL DOWN THE CELLAR...YOU CAN BE BOSS DOWN THERE... AND I'M BOSS DOWN HERE...AND YOU AIN'T TAKIN' NONE OF THIS FOOD, AND YOU AIN'T TAKIN' NOTHIN'".

TOM: "HARRY...WE CAN GET FOOD TO YOU...IF YOU WANT TO STAY DOWN THERE...AND..."

HARRY: "YOU BASTARDS!"

HELEN: (from the cellar): "HARRY...HARRY!"

Harry looks toward the cellar door, looks back at the two men, then quickly moves toward the door.

HARRY: "YOU KNOW I WON'T OPEN THE DOOR AGAIN. I MEAN IT."

TOM: "WE CAN FIX THIS UP HERE. WITH YOUR HELP, WE COULD..."

HARRY: "YEAH...WELL I THINK YOU'RE BOTH NUTS...WITH MY HELP!..."

TRUCKDRIVER: (to Tom) "LET HIM GO, MAN, HIS MIND IS MADE UP, NOW LET HIM GO."

Harry looks for a moment, then lunges for the cellar door, opens it, and slams it behind him...sounds of his footsteps going down the steps...

TOM: (rushes to the door) "HARRY, WE'D BE BETTER OFF UP HERE!"

The truckdriver ties the broken fringe back onto the rifle, then begins to reload the gun, replacing the spent shells.

TOM: (shouting through the door) "HARRY, IF WE STICK TOGETHER, MAN, WE CAN FIX IT UP REAL GOOD...THERE ARE PLACES WE CAN RUN TO

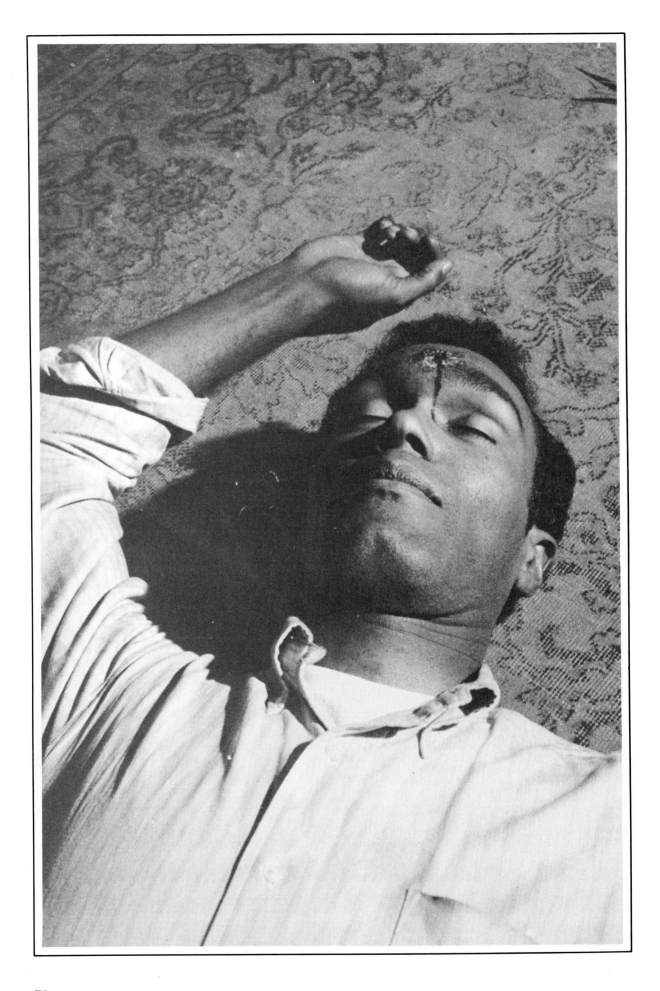

A WORD FROM THE PRODUCERS: RUSSELL W. STREINER AND KARL HARDMAN

"NIGHT OF THE LIVING DEAD has a little of everything to satisfy most customers. There's the gore, the flowing blood. There's violence galore. There's an uncompromising ending that leaves most viewers dumbfounded. There's even a nude...before nudes were popular in horror films. In the last analysis, this unique film succeeded because it was the kind of film audiences hungered for. Simply, it was the right movie to come along at the right time. And it was honest. What it promised its audience, it gave them in full measure, even far exceeding most expectations."

—Gary Anthony Surmacz, Cinefantastique

Gary Anthony Surmacz conducted the following interview for *Cinefantastique Magazine.** The quote above is from his preface. I was part of the interview, along with Russ and Karl, but here I have abridged the article and edited my comments out. I have had enough to say in the rest of this book, and did not wish to be redundant. And I wanted to give Russ and Karl their say, because I'm sure that fans of NIGHT OF THE LIVING DEAD will be interested.

CFQ: Why did you choose a horror film for your first venture? Is it because it is the easiest film to make, and the easiest to sell?

HARDMAN: I think we all agreed it would be the most commercial film we could produce.

STREINER: And let's face it, it was the first feature any of us had been involved in. I think Karl might have been involved in something on the West Coast years back, but certainly not in the role of producer. And frankly, we had to do the kind of picture that we were almost assured of being able to sell. A horror film seemed to fit the bill. We did not have a distribution deal when we started into production. We did it on our money and our investors' money, and then secured the distribution deal.

CFQ: In the beginning, was the film intended to be done under the aegis of a separate corporation or by the existing Latent Image?

STREINER: It was intended to be made under a separate corporation. There were several inherent problems had we done it as a Latent Image project. It got into a big stock hassle and things like that, so we chose the path of least resistance and that was to set up a

separate corporation and then sell shares in the corporation. Latent Image, as a corporation, owns no stock in Image Ten.

CFQ: In what ways was the final NIGHT OF THE LIVING DEAD different than what you had originally planned, if it was at all?

STREINER: Well, let's face it. We're dealing with a fantasy premise, but deep down inside we were all serious filmmakers and somewhat disappointed because we had to resort to horror for our first film. I mean everyone would like to do the great American film, but we found ourselves, through a series of what we thought were logical conclusions, making a horror film. Once we adopted that for openers, we then tried to make the best, most realistic horror film that we could make on the money we had available. In all aspects of the production we treated it as a serious film, although sometimes it's hard to treat that kind of premise seriously. I think that overriding viewpoint is displayed in the final product. Once you buy the fact that the dead come back to life, it's treated in all other regards as a serious film.

CFQ: Your use of the television was very good.

HARDMAN: Yes. The premise, of course, was the Venus probe being sent out and on return picking up some stray radiation. The radiation was detected and the probe exploded, with chunks falling into the earth's atmosphere. That, naturally, would spread it over a fairly large piece of real estate.

STREINER: There was some discussion as to whether the phenomenon needed to be explored that deeply. Did we even have to reveal how the phenomenon came to be? There was

*Reprinted by permission of both the author and CINEFANTASTIQUE.

some discussion about that, and then we settled for the compromise—the old radiation trick.

CFQ: Don't you think it would have been interesting if no possible explanation were given?

HARDMAN: It was safer to explain it. That was the only conclusion.

CFQ: Is NIGHT OF THE LIVING DEAD an allegory?

STREINER: I think in setting out to make a general entertainment film, if some critics were entertained to the point that they began reading all these fantastic social implications into it, fine, if that's how they're entertained. But I can't say that there were any overriding social ramifications in the original design of the film. In all honesty, I would have to say that with as many of the production's shortcomings as we can attribute to budget, and there were a lot of those, you have to remember that it's the first feature we had ever completed. We had normal production headaches that we had experience at before.

We learned an awful lot from the whole experience, down through the distribution arrangement. There are a lot of things that we would now never consider doing on another picture, either in terms of the production schedule or the distribution agreement.

CFQ: Were the ghouls in the original concept? Were the living dead intended to eat human flesh?

STREINER: They were ghouls. The original title was THE FLESHEATERS. Insofar as the gore is concerned, I can recall that at the time there seemed to be a very heavy influx of so-called horror films...

HARDMAN: That was the time of BLOOD FEAST.

STREINER: ...that were made in Mexico and other foreign countries. They were just abominable. They were just terrible films in every sense of the word. They had no terror value, and almost no value, period. We decided that once we reconciled ourselves to that premise then why sell it out? If we presume that the recently dead were coming back to

Johnny comes back from the dead for Barbara

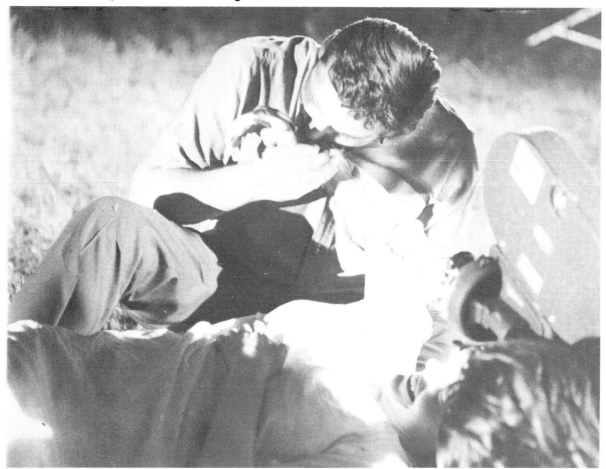

life and would maim and otherwise devour victims, then let's show it. I think in that sense, that's the reason the film caught on so well. It didn't sell out. A lot of people got sick, but when girls went to the drive-ins with their boyfriends, they ended up hiding their faces a lot. I think it has a value. In that context, in that film, I think it worked.

HARDMAN: I think one of the reasons, luckily for us, that the thing went that way was because we couldn't afford to fabricate sets. We couldn't build a monster. These things were not available to us. We just couldn't do it. We had to do it with human beings.

STREINER: Getting back to the question you asked earlier about allegory in the film. A lot of people have read in some meaning to the casting of Duane Jones, a black, playing the male lead. The simple truth of the matter is that he just turned out to be the best person for the part. He would have gotten the part if he were an Oriental or an American Indian or an Eskimo.

CFQ: The casting of Jones, and the ending, which is so defeating in a sense, are probably the reasons the film has caught on. You can't deny the reaction whether accidental or not.

HARDMAN: I had a third ending. Remember that? I wanted to have everything wrapped up. Duane shot. All the ghouls wiped out. And then I wanted to have the little girl step into the frame as the posse drives away in the distance, watching the posse disappear. To have one ghoul left.

STREINER: You see, we could kick the ending of NIGHT OF THE LIVING DEAD back and forth, and we could kick the gore back and forth, but somehow all of those ingredients went into—and I don't think I'm being a braggard about it—creating a memorable film. It certainly ranks with the films that are going to be around for a while. So we obviously did something right, even though we could probably nitpick and second-guess a lot of the specifics about the film.

CFQ: You mentioned that the original title of the film was THE FLESHEATERS. What were some of the other titles considered?

HARDMAN: NIGHT OF ANUBIS was considered for a long time. But Anubis was so obscure.

STREINER: Yes, a little too esoteric for the film.

CFQ: How many years has it played in midnight showings in what cities?

STREINER: Well, that's happened in Boston, New York and Philadelphia.

HARDMAN: Two years straight in Minneapolis.

75

STREINER: It's also interesting that NIGHT OF THE LIVING DEAD has not been out of distribution. That's why it doesn't have a rating.

CFQ: When you have the chance, do you sneak into the back of a theater where the film is playing?

STREINER: As a matter of fact, the opening night of the film, the night after the premiere, I went by myself to a predominantly black theater in a black neighborhood. That's an experience in itself. It's amazing how much blacks are entertained by that picture. I've never quite seen anything like it in terms of audience involvement. People were standing on their feet and shouting instructions to the characters.

CFQ: What was the reaction of the black audience to the end of the film? Was the audience taken aback by this?

STREINER: Oh yes, and also very angry about it. You could hear murmurings of, "Well, you know, they had to kill him off!" and "Whitey had to get him anyway!" and "He bought it from the Man." Maybe the whole feeling would be different if, for instance, Superman had been black. I think the black community is looking for a latter day Superman. They found him in SHAFT and they find him in Ben. It's really kind of gratifying to know that something you've had a hand in has some impact on people. Especially when you've come from a background of making TV commercials.

CFQ: Both of you, Russ and Karl, played various roles in the making of the film. Both of you acted in the picture: Karl playing Harry Cooper and Russ playing Johnny, the girl's brother. Did you find any problems in terms of acting conflicting with your behind-the-scenes work?

STREINER: Well, in my case, you noticed I was killed off in the first five minutes. I think that had something to say about my performance. I was uptight about it. You can stroll around behind the camera and you have an ability to tell people how you want to see something, but when you're on the receiving end, as far as I'm concerned, it's a totally different matter.

CFQ: Karl, you were prominent in the film. Did you have any problems?

HARDMAN: Yes I did, as a matter of fact. Duane Jones, in my personal view and only my personal view, was underplaying far, far too much. He was too far down. And that

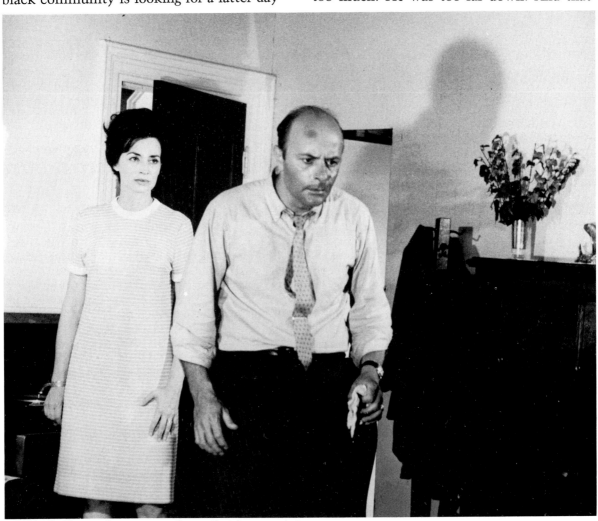

Helen & Harry Cooper up from the basement

76

worried me because I thought there had to be some inflection in the film. I guess we talked about that generally and some agreed, others didn't. But I decided that my character should be a sharp contrast with Duane's character. So I played Harry Cooper in a kind of frenzied, fist-clenching, nervous way. And when the first rushes came back and I saw myself on the screen it was really embarrassing because, to me, Harry Cooper came off like a comic opera figure.

STREINER: Well, didn't you move to Buenos Aires for a while after that?

HARDMAN: (chuckles) Yes. I felt I had to get out of town.

CFQ: The scene that impressed me most in the entire film was the opening scene, with the car driving along the road.

HARDMAN: It's ominous.

CFQ: Right away you said to yourself that something was wrong all around. It was just so well done. How did you approach the distributors with this film?

STREINER: With a great deal of trepidation. We finished the picture and George Romero and I were driving to New York on the night Martin Luther King was assassinated. And we figured, oh, great, everything else has gone wrong up to this point and here we show up with a film where a black man plays the lead and *also* gets killed, and besides, probably every theater in the country is going to be burned down within two days. We were not successful with our first attempt with the picture. Columbia Pictures had it for quite some time.

CFQ: Were they the first ones?

STREINER: They were the first ones to see the picture. In any event, Columbia had the picture tied up for quite some time, all the time giving us encouraging words like, "Yes, we like the picture," and "It's just going through another battery of screenings," and things like that. I came back to Pittsburgh and George stayed there for a couple of days. But we were satisfied that the picture was going to Columbia. Then George called us a few days later and said that Columbia eventually turned it down. At that point we started looking around for a producer's representative. We figured our inexperience apparently must be showing through to these people. So we needed and secured a producer's rep. After the rep picked up the picture we had five offers that were almost identical over the next two months or so. We finally went with Walter Reade.

CFQ: What kind of deal does an independent producer get with a major distributor?

STREINER: We had a fifty-fifty deal. The prints and advertising came off the top and then everything after that was to be split fifty-fifty.

CFQ: While actually filming, did you do anything to attract distributors?

STREINER: The only thing we did during production was to round up an awful lot of production shots and we did put together a press kit of sorts, or a publicity kit with a dozen photographs and a few other things and sent it around to various distributors while the picture was being edited. It got very little response.

CFQ: In respect to the Reade Organization, was there any agreement made for future films?

STREINER: No. At the time we were looking for money to do another picture and Walter Reade offered, and, in fact, got approved from the Bank of America a letter of credit for some fifty thousand dollars. And after the letter of credit was issued they attempted to secure an agreement from us that other pictures we did could be distributed by Reade on the same terms as NIGHT OF THE LIVING DEAD. We turned down the letter of credit and the attached agreement.

CFQ: Let's discuss the first test screening of the film. What was the general reaction of the audience? Who was there?

HARDMAN: They were largely friends. People who had been in it or had heard about it but hadn't seen it. Everyone was given cards asking for written opinions of the film. In fact, after a couple of those screenings, it was decided to eliminate a lot of the exposition, which is the slow part of the film. The Venus probe and what's going on in this part of the country and that part of the country were all radically reduced in length.

A NOLD poster from Germany

STREINER: After we finished the film we went into a period of deep depression.

HARDMAN: When you make a film, even though you go into it with the intellectual point of view that you may bomb out, and you're completely willing to bomb out, and what right do you have to hit with this when there are so many films being made by so many important people that don't make it, you still think that it's got to go. It's going to be good enough. It'll sell. People will dig it. So it's that really "on top" feeling.

CFQ: You were, I would imagine, somewhat surprised at the critical response to the film?

HARDMAN: Everyone knows about the film. The longer this film stays in distribution and the more I hear about this cult and that cult, the more astounded I become that we made this film. I'm delighted, I might add.

CFQ: Would you consider this film, because of the response it's getting, somewhat of an "art" film?

HARDMAN: Art film? No.

STREINER: No. I wouldn't consider it that way. I think it's a flat-out entertainment picture and people who enjoy films will continue to be entertained by it. I don't think you can all of a sudden say that because a lot of people are interested in seeing this picture it is an art film. It's a film that pays off most people. It has some value other than the blood and guts aspect.

CFQ: Was there any crisis before or during the making of the film?

STREINER: The only crisis was keeping the commode at the location working. That created some very tense, anxiety-filled moments. Other than that I shot Karl in the chest three or four times. My brother got his arm burned one night...while we were shooting one of the outdoor scenes.

CFQ: Was your script completed when you began shooting?

STREINER: It was completed. Once the shooting started to take some shape, the script was embellished, but the basic script was finished when we started shooting.

CFQ: I read that the scene Karl so fondly refers to as "The Last Supper" was a spur of the moment addition. Didn't a butcher drive onto the set with all those intestines?

HARDMAN: Well, no. One of the stockholders owned a chain of meat markets. We knew that we needed intestines, livers, hearts and stuff like that. So he arranged to get those things from the slaughter house from which he purchased meat. They were all goodies belonging to lambs which are supposedly similar to human organs. We had to slush out the intestines, literally. That was pretty grim. By the way, I'm still amazed that somebody during the filming didn't just collapse and die, right on the spot.

CFQ: Why do you say that?

HARDMAN: Because of the hours.

STREINER: I don't think we'd go through the same kind of production schedule again. At four o'clock in the morning, after you've been working eighteen hours, your objectivity gets a little on the cloudy side, and all you're interested in doing is sacking out someplace. You've been living on ham and cheese sandwiches and a couple of beers for three days.

CFQ: You used local, non-professional people in this film for supporting roles and as the ghouls. What was the reaction when you walked up to somebody and told them, "What we want you to do is wear these torn clothes and munch on these animal intestines"?

HARDMAN: Both Latent Image and Hardman Associates were working closely with all the advertising agencies in the city. The word was out that this picture was going to be made. We simply put out the word that we needed extras and everyone, almost without exception, was very eager to take part.

CFQ: Were these people paid for what they did?

HARDMAN: Ultimately, everyone was paid.

STREINER: There was a fair amount of interest, too, in Evans City about the shooting itself. Like the night we blew up the truck. We had two identical trucks. One we rented up there. Didn't we buy the other one for around forty-five dollars?

HARDMAN: Yes, something like that.

STREINER: We towed it up there. On the night we blew up the truck we decided to wait until two o'clock in the morning because we weren't quite sure what was going to happen. Still, there must've been 100 to 150 people who hung around. They wouldn't go home.

CFQ: Did anything happen that you didn't expect?

STREINER: No. It was just that everyone was so curious. I just mention the truck blowing up, but there were nights when people would hang around way into the morning hours just out of sheer curiosity.

HARDMAN: When you're dealing with pyrotechnics and you're not quite sure as to what will happen, a hubcap could sail off and decapitate someone.

CFQ: What was the hardest scene you had to shoot? Karl, I remember something about a coat tree that kept following you down the stairs?

HARDMAN: From my own personal point of view that was the hardest.

STREINER: Karl's famous death.

CFQ: Would you elaborate on that?

HARDMAN: Very simply, I was holding a

The Final Siege—Helen in terror

rifle on Duane and saying we were going to do things my way. He turned and threw a board at me, knocking the rifle out of my hands. He grabbed the rifle, leveled it—whamm! The force of the bullet was to slam me into the corner. I was to bounce off the corner, hit the piano on the other side of the doorway leading to the basement, then, clutching myself, fall down the steps into the basement of the house. Well, there was a coat tree next to the door which had been in every shot, and there were coats on it. Eleven times I got shot, slammed myself into the corner, bounced off onto the piano and got wrapped up in that coat tree, and the coat tree would follow me into the basement. By the time we got a good take I was so exhausted from laughing I hardly had enough energly left to do it.

STREINER: Probably the most difficult shooting was the day we photographed most of the posse, the helicopters and the police dogs. It was difficult just from a pure logistics point of view. We had an awful lot of people to handle. We also had to be very careful. One person was assigned to make sure all of the live ammunition was out of the weapons being used in the scene and replaced with blanks. We didn't want any mishaps, or anybody thinking they had an empty gun and, in fact, shooting someone. That was difficult, but only in the sense of the logistics.

Ghouls attack en masse

CFQ: It is very difficult to assign creative credit to a cooperative effort such as film-making. Who deserves the credit for whatever success NIGHT OF THE LIVING DEAD has achieved?

STREINER: It's hard to say where the success really lies. Is it in the original concept or is it in the collective attitude with which the project was approached? George Romero certainly deserves a lot of the credit. There was a core of maybe five or six people who were all ultimately responsible for the success of the film and I'm not trying to add or detract credit from any one person by saying that. But in my opinion, that's the way it is.

HARDMAN: I agree with what Russ has said. I think if I had to enumerate key people so far as the actual production itself, certainly George Romero, John Russo, Russ Streiner—I'm thinking of whole areas in which these people worked—myself, Marilyn Eastman, and, I think, Vince Survinski.

STREINER: Yes, very definitely. Vince is one of the guys who generally is always in the background and almost never gets any publicity. He's just as happy that way.

CFQ: Do either of you have an inclination toward making horror films?

HARDMAN: I do. I think they're fun.

STREINER: I think there's a large enough audience for films like NIGHT OF THE LIVING DEAD. If people can be entertained by it, then there's a value in making such a picture.

CFQ: There is much said about horror films giving people a release from their

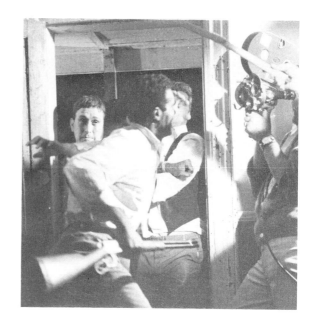

frustrations. Some have called them healthy outlets. Do you have any thoughts on this?

HARDMAN: I think if you say horror films are healthy it's only because the people are entertained and it provides them release.

CFQ: Good always wins out over Evil in fairy tales. But there are many horror films today where that just doesn't happen, or there is no clear-cut sense of good and evil. In NIGHT OF THE LIVING DEAD there is no clear definition of good and evil.

STREINER: NIGHT OF THE LIVING

DEAD had been out for maybe a year when a story appeared in *Life* magazine. It just so happened at the time, in some small town in Nebraska, a parent group was up in arms that the owner of the only theater in their community opted to play films like NIGHT OF THE LIVING DEAD. Their complaint was that he had a captive audience and if people in that small town wanted to go to the theater they had to see what the owner thought they should see. But I can't help thinking that when you drop your kid off in front of the show and the marquee says NIGHT OF THE LIVING DEAD, you should know it isn't going to be a Disney film or HANS BRINKER AND THE SILVER SKATES.

CFQ: What horror films have you seen that impressed you?

STREINER: In its time, THE THING terrified me. PSYCHO is one of my all-time favorites. INVASION OF THE BODY SNATCHERS was a good film. There are several science fiction films, some of the things George Pal did, and there was THE DAY THE EARTH STOOD STILL. That was a good film. VILLAGE OF THE DAMNED also had something going for it.

HARDMAN: I was going to mention FRANKENSTEIN, THE PHANTOM OF THE OPERA, and DRACULA. That places me at a

point in time when I was very young and they really scared me.

STREINER: I'm more in favor of the Hitchcock brand of suspense and terror than the overt, blatant terror. If you can trigger the audience's imagination, you've won the battle. You can't do everything for them. You've got to trip something in their personal psychology if you want them to laugh, cry or be frightened.

CFQ: Well, there's only one other thing I don't understand. It's that clothes pole that kept following you down the stairs, Karl. It amazes me that all those people in that farmhouse, their lives in horrifying danger, would take time out to hang up their coats!

82

POST-PRODUCTION:
THE PIECES COME TOGETHER

"That film was shot over a period of about nine months, with great breaks in between to come back and do a pickle commercial or something, which was distressing. After we got some footage in the can where we could screen rushes for people, people started coming 'round saying, Hey, that looks like a movie! And we said, Well that's what it is!"

—George A. Romero

George made the above statements in a *Cinefantastique* interview a few years ago. He was describing the ingrained reluctance of people—including some of our friends, families and relatives—to believe that a "real movie" could be made by a bunch of young guys in Pittsburgh. NIGHT OF THE LIVING DEAD went a long ways toward changing all that.

It was November 1967 when we shot the graveyard scenes. Over the winter of 1967-1968, in between commercial gigs, we worked on synching takes, recording sound effects, and editing. The takes were synched by George Romero, Gary Streiner, Judith Ridley (who was now working for The Latent Image), and myself. I think George Kosana pitched in, too. Many of the sound effects were done by Karl Hardman, Marilyn Eastman and others at Hardman Associates. Gary, Russ and I also contributed. I remember that the sound of the tire iron stabbing my head was made by stabbing a honeydew melon.

George Romero did all of the rough-cutting and polished editing, a mammoth task—and a fine job. Once he bagged into it, he wouldn't let go, and worked himself into near total exhaustion. The group of us would screen the edits, discuss them, and arrive at suggestions for changes, if any. But George was such an excellent editor that he mostly carried the weight on his own shoulders.

One of our big stumbling blocks was music—where to get it, and how to get it cheaply. Over a period of a couple of weeks during the rough-cut stage, we had some pretty wild and zany sessions, trying to create our own weird music even though none of us were musicians. But we had The Latent Image's recording studio available, with Gary Streiner as recording engineer. We "worked out" on drums, plucked guitar strings, banged cymbals, and made eerie noises with our own voices—and even with things like ratchets and drills—while Gary experimented with reverb, or tried running some of the sounds backwards after they were recorded. Some of this crazy stuff actually got used in bits and pieces on the effects tracks of the Monster Flick. Karl and Marilyn created some sounds that got used more extensively.

We went through all this trouble because we really didn't want to use library music—we wanted an original score. We didn't think we could find enough good library selections to score an entire horror movie and do it well. Then, as another alternative, or shot in the dark, we tried to buy the rights to the JACK THE RIPPER score to use parts of it in our movie. But the licensors wanted too much money; either that, or they didn't wish to license it, I forget which.

Finally, we ended up using the Capitol Hi-Q library. Karl Hardman and George Romero made such great selections that our music track ended up being quite successful—in fact, most fans and critics consider it a tremendous boon to the film. Recently we released a sound-track album of NIGHT OF THE LIVING DEAD, produced by Scot Holton on Varese-Sarabande Records. Here are some zesty comments George Romero wrote for the back of the album:

"Karl Hardman and the Capitol Hi-Q Library to the rescue. Karl's production company had the library discs in house and he began to make preliminary picks. We listened and were delighted with the music. This was the real article. The scoring heard in nightmares conjured by yesterday's matinees. If the boogieman had a ghetto-blaster, this was the stuff he'd boogie to.''

During the post-production period, as Russ Streiner said in the preceding chapter, there was a point when we ''sank into a deep depression.'' I don't think it was quite *that* bad. But it was certainly a malaise. It was the let-down after a flurry of insanely demanding activity, when the adrenaline stops flowing all of a sudden and you find yourself completely wrung-out.

But being able to see lip-synch takes perked us up again. We started to realize anew the value of what we had accomplished during filming. And, as the work progressed from rough-cuts to a finished edit, we knew for sure that we had a damned good movie. A feeling of exhilaration set in. We had been down, but now we were back up.

By the way, we did all of our editing in 16-millimeter instead of 35. We had all of the 35-millimeter negative reduction workprinted to 16 because all of the equipment we owned for our commercial work—editing, dubbing and mixing—was 16-millimeter equipment.

We held our first big screening of the complete movie in interlock format—sound and picture tracks run synchronously on separate machines, because they weren't printed together yet on one piece of film—in March of 1968 in The Latent Image's downstairs studio. The place was overflowing with shareholders, actors and friends. My wife Mary Lou (we were not married then) saw the picture that day for the first time. I knew it was having the desired effect on her when she clenched my hand so tightly and so many times during ''scary scenes'' that I thought she was going to break my fingers. Everybody present was stunned by the movie—by its raw power and terror. This was a reaction that was to repeat and repeat itself in years to come, with audiences all over the world.

But we still had to sell the picture first. And we weren't totally sure that we could get a distribution deal. As I pointed out before, we had no experience with the major distributors or the independents. What if they didn't want our product for some reason, even though *we* knew it was a good picture?

We decided *not* to try to sell by screening the interlock for distributors, which would've been the cheapest thing to do. At

this point, convinced that our movie was special, we wished to give it every possible advantage in the market place. This meant that we had to come up with some way of paying for a finished 35-millimeter print—and of course Image Ten was out of money.

Nevertheless, not to waste time, Gary Streiner and I started conforming the picture: matching the 16-millimeter edit to the 35-millimeter negative, and splicing the shots together in what is known as a "checkerboard" pattern for printing. There were over a thousand shots. This represented several weeks of painstaking work, since a 16-35 synchronizer had to be used, and it is very easy to scratch 35-millimeter negative if one isn't extremely careful.

Meanwhile, Russ Streiner made a deal with Jack Napor, president of WRS Motion Picture Laboratory, to put the costs of the 35-millimeter print on The Latent Image's lab bill—with extended credit. This was after we screened the interlock for Jack Napor and he was impressed with our movie's commercial potential. After this meeting, George,

Russ, Jack Napor and I went out drinking—and got to feeling pretty good. In the midst of the celebrating, we found ourselves in a bar where the tabletops were chess boards, and chess pieces were available for the customers. Russ and Jack got into a slurred debate over which one was the better chess player, and Russ challenged Jack to a game. They haggled over the stakes, which turned out to be very *high* and scary for us at that time:

If Russ won, WRS Motion Picture Laboratory would do all of our finished mixing and sound-track printing for free. But if Jack Napor won, we'd have to pay double.

On pins and needles, George and I drank beer and watched Russ and Jack move chess pieces in a contest of wit and strategy, or at least it might have been that, if they were sober.

Russ ended up winning! And Jack Napor kept his word. It was a tremendous victory that night for Image Ten, considering our dire financial straits. The work that was done for free was worth about two thousand dollars.

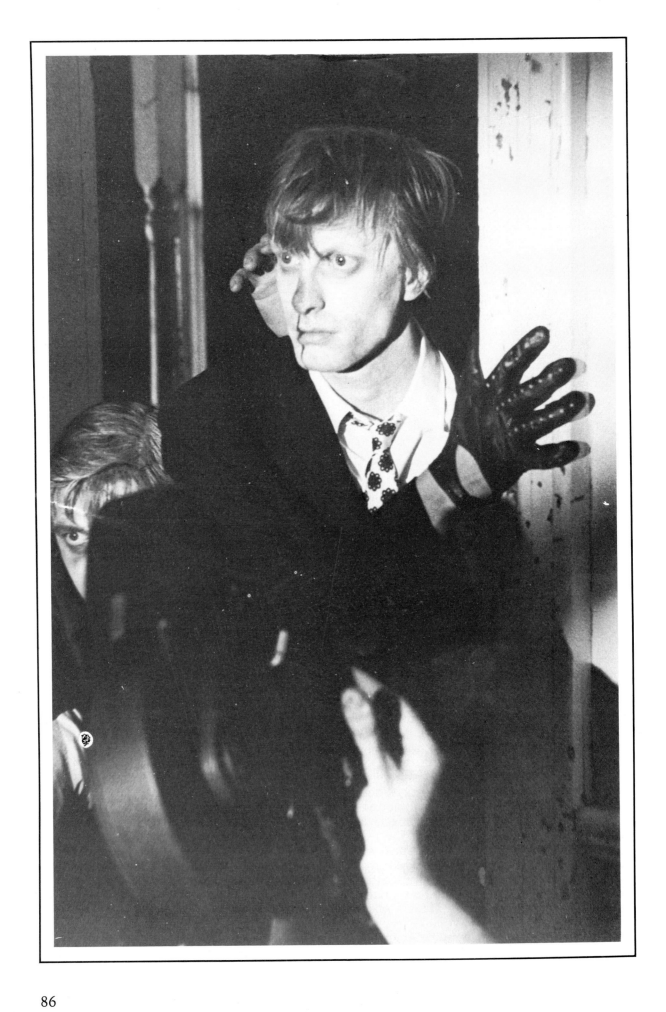

THE MONSTER FLICK GOES TO MARKET

"American International turned the picture down on the basis of it being too unmitigating. They told us that if we would reshoot the end of it they would distribute it. Have Ben survive and come out somehow."
—George A. Romero, Cinefantastique

George Romero and Russ Streiner came back from New York depressed because every single distributor they screened the film for told them it was AIP's type of picture all the way, and then AIP didn't take it. It seemed like the picture really might not get sold. We were at a loss as to why. Was there a distributors' establishment that outsiders just couldn't crack, or what? I decided to phone Sam Arkoff, president of AIP, and ask him directly why his company didn't want our film. He was very nice to me, and we had a fairly long conversation. He explained that AIP couldn't distribute every picture that came along; they only had a budget for a certain number of pictures in their release schedule, and the schedule was filled up. They had almost decided to squeeze one more in, anyway, but then the vote of their executives had narrowly gone the other way.

Well, getting it "from the horse's mouth" made us feel better. All was not lost. One important thing that George and Russ had accomplished was to land a producer's representative in New York, a man in his late sixties with forty years' experience in the distribution business, Budd Rogers. Budd assured us that our picture would get distributed; he would be able to negotiate a deal.

While George was in New York, he had telephoned me as I was having dinner with my parents in Clairton. "Well, Jack," he had said excitedly, "it looks like the flick is going to the Lady with the Torch." He meant Columbia, of course. Actually, they came very close to offering us a deal. After numerous screenings for their sales staff and promotions people, the picture got turned down mainly because it was in black-and-white. The vast majority of pictures were going out in color during this period, for the first time in the industry's history. This was because of the de-vastating inroads of television. Putting wide-screen color in the theaters was a way of competing with the little black-and-white tubes in most people's homes. Also, the drive-in market was more important than ever, and we were told that black-and-white pictures didn't have enough resolution over the long distance from projector to screen in the huge drive-ins, and so could not be shown in the hours of dusk, before the sun was completely down.

We were beginning to "get our feet wet" and to learn distribution and marketing considerations that had never occurred to us before.

However, to our great relief, within a short time Budd Rogers was able to obtain five offers for our picture. They were all virtually identical, and all from relatively small, independent distributors. The basic deal was a fifty-fifty split after deducting the cost of advertising and prints. What we did not sufficiently recognize at the time, because of our naivete regarding distribution, was how *exceptional* it was to have a low-budget picture almost bought by a major studio and to have, not just one, but *five* offers from the independents. Usually, any picture is lucky to get just one offer, and the vast majority of pictures—hundreds of them, in fact—sit on shelves without ever finding an audience. We had accomplished something extraordinary our first time out of the gate, but we didn't know this, and so we had been more worried than we needed to be.

After some weeks of negotiation with the various companies making offers, Budd Rogers recommended that we go with Continental Pictures, the motion picture distribution branch of the Walter Reade Organization, which was also into film exhibition, production and many other enterprises. We thought that Continental would be a good choice, too. In fact, we felt somewhat honored that our picture would be handled by a distributor mainly noted for "art house" product such as FACES, DAVID AND LISA, LORD OF THE FLIES, and ROOM AT THE TOP. With NIGHT OF THE LIVING DEAD, Continental was for the first time taking on an exploitation picture, and we thought that said something for the quality of our work.

Russ Streiner and I went to New York to discuss details of the contract that was being formulated, with officers of Continental Pictures and The Walter Reade Organization. Budd Rogers was present, as were Jerry Pickman, the president of Continental, and Harold Marenstein, the national sales manager. We worked out basic contractual considerations, and a document was drawn up and later reviewed by the officers of Image Ten and Image Ten's attorney, Dave Clipper.

When we were back in Pittsburgh, after the contract was signed, we were asked to produce television and radio spots for our picture, and to contribute ideas for the press book that the distribution company would put together. Jerry Pickman and Harold Marenstein met with us several times to hash out ideas and select stills that would become part of the "official packet" for theater lobbies. At around this time, the final title of the film was arrived at: NIGHT OF THE LIVING DEAD.

NOTE: We had a list hanging on a bulletin board at The Latent Image where people would write down title suggestions. My suggestion was SOUTH PACIFIC, but for some reason it got vetoed.

George Romero and I worked at writing

copy and pulling material from our movie that could go into the television commercials. We then made a series of ten-, twenty-, thirty-, and sixty-second spots for radio and TV, and I believe we made a preview trailer, with George doing the editing.

But the advertising department at Continental thought our stuff wasn't hard-sell enough. So they did some re-editing and used a different narrator with a ''spooky'' Boris Karloff style. However, a lead line I wrote—''pits the dead against the living in a struggle for survival''—remained a key line in the spots and the press book, which was at least some consolation for all the hard work.

Continental also wanted five or six minutes cut out of NIGHT OF THE LIVING DEAD in some of the scenes that they considered slow-moving, and they wanted more cannibalism scenes put in, if possible. We didn't have many shots of the ghouls feasting that we had not already used, but we were able to scrape up a couple. George Romero talked about these changes in an interview in *Cinefantastique*: ''I had expansive shots of the fields with just the ghouls dotting the countryside, which I felt at that point would have been more effective, but the distributor insisted that we cut back to the ghouls eating flesh. I said, no, we've had that, but of course, I didn't get my way.''

Here is also where, in getting the 35-millimeter negative ready for the lab, I made the jump-cut talked about earlier, which George absolutely hated. But it was the only way to shorten the scene.

All of this activity—getting our first movie in shape for international distribution—was very exciting, even exhilarating. We were anxious for the big event to actually take place. But the months kept trickling away without any formal release date being set. We kept pressing the distributor to get going.

Finally, Continental decided to test-market NIGHT OF THE LIVING DEAD right in our home city—and to once again enlist our support. In other words, they were taking the easiest and cheapest way out for themselves. If the picture bombed on our turf, they could quietly pull it out of release and cut their losses.

THE WORLD PREMIERE: LIMOUSINES AND KLIEG LIGHTS

"NIGHT OF THE LIVING DEAD had its world premiere at the Fulton Theater last night and even shook up the hardiest of chiller-thriller fans. Some of the scenes are so grisly that...it's a gourmet session for those followers of macabre, grotesque situations. A rouser for the strong-stomached horror film addict."

—*Thomas Blakely, The Pittsburgh Press*

We took it upon ourselves to try and make sure our movie didn't bomb in Pittsburgh. Our hope was that if we could produce big enough box-office grosses, the distribution would expand to other major cities. It was a far cry from the sort of "national distribution" we had hoped for, but we had to face the situation and make the most of it.

What we were facing, and learning about in detail for the first time, was the difference between the way the independent distributors had to operate, compared to the majors.

When a major—such as Columbia, Universal, or United Artists—opens a picture, it goes into what is called "key run" release, which means that it will debut in roughly a thousand of the best-grossing theaters all across America, and all at the same time. Over a thousand prints will be pulled, at a cost of about one thousand dollars apiece, for a total of around a million dollars. On top of this, there will be a tremendous advertising campaign, involving network TV spots, etc., which will cost, say, another two or three million dollars. The picture gets tremendous "exposure." If it hits, it can gross an enormous amount of money and do it quickly because of "saturation" advertising and booking, not to mention the hefty advances theaters often have to fork out to acquire key-run pictures.

The independent distributor—such as Continental—cannot pay out three to five million dollars for prints and advertising on a picture. So he distributes on a regional basis, pulling, say, fifteen to thirty prints, and making cooperative advertising deals with the theater chains in the cities where he can get his picture played. This means that the cost of advertising comes off the top of the box-office receipts, and the distributor gets a percentage of the remainder, which is usually a *low* percentage, around 25%, but can be higher, depending on how well the picture does. If it does well, he can move it from region to region across the country, perhaps pulling additional prints so he can book more theaters in each territory or play more than one territory at a time.

I might point out that in some cases, for blockbuster pictures, the majors take up to *90%* of the box-office gross. Besides producing big-budget pictures with big-name stars, they can offer a continual supply of "hot" product that the theater owners must clamor after.

So, to summarize, the independent distributor (and producer) suffers in a number of ways, including:
(1) Inadequate advertising.
(2) Not enough prints to distribute on a large scale.
(3) Low percentage of the profits.
(4) Playing the low-grossing neighborhood or drive-in theaters instead of key-run houses.
(5) Taking months and months to move a small number of prints from place to place instead of bombarding the whole country at once.
(6) Not collecting money for a long time because of the slowness of the independent distribution process. This ties up potential profits and slows investment in new product.

What this all boiled down to was that if NIGHT OF THE LIVING DEAD didn't make a big enough splash in Pittsburgh, it might fade away into obscurity. We were determined to contribute our utmost toward the success of our own picture. Our mode of operation had always been to go all-out whenever anything important was at stake. We took pride in our reputation for trying our best at every job that came along, even if it was only a 30-second TV spot for some client who couldn't afford to pay top dollar. We certainly didn't want to drop the ball now, when our future as producers of theatrical features might depend on it. If for some reason our picture didn't make it at the box office, we didn't want to have to sit around and wonder if maybe the outcome would've been different if we had put forth more effort.

Russ Streiner and I took charge of the local advertising and promotion campaign—with plenty of back-up support from everybody involved with the picture. One of the "little things" we did, which I think had some impact, was to have one thousand copies of the NIGHT OF THE LIVING DEAD one-sheet (poster) printed up, which were distributed to shareholders and friends, who then posted them on bulletin boards, telephone poles, store fronts, office walls, etc. It made everybody feel involved. And it got lots of attention for our movie wherever throngs of people

DON'T
TAKE
OUR
WORD
FOR IT...

READ
WHAT
FILM
DAILY
SAYS!

REVIEW OF NEW FILM

'NIGHT OF THE LIVING DEAD'

with Judith O'Dea, Duane Jones, Russell Streiner, Karl Hardman
Continental Distributing

90 Mins.

GEM OF HORROR PICTURE POSSESSES ALL THE EARMARKS OF A "SLEEPER." STRONG STUFF FOR DELICATE STOMACHS.

With "Night of the Living Dead" Image Ten, a new Pittsburgh company, starts off with a wallop as a producer of theatrical motion pictures. This is a pearl of a horror picture which exhibits all the earmarks of a "sleeper." Accorded the right exploitation, it could make a whale of a boxoffice showing. At times the film is shocking in its display of the horrible. Those with quesy stomach will find some of what goes on in the picture hard to take. There is a number of scenes that are certain to startle the audience. Not many films have been able to create so vivid a sense of terror. There are a number of scenes that perhaps go too far in their realism.

The story, into the telling of which much imagination, resourcefulness and inventiveness have gone, has to do with an attack upon the living by ghouls triggered into action by the effects of atomic radiation upon their brains. The terrifying thing about these walking dead is that they devour any living person they encounter.

The first indication of what the audience is in for comes when Russell Streiner becomes the victim of a ghoul in a cemetery visit with Judith O'Dea, his sister. She, along with others menaced by the ghouls, takes refuge in a farmhouse. Among those boxed in with her are Duane Jones and Karl Hardman.

Most of the action touches on the frantic efforts of those in the house to make the place secure against invasion by the ghouls. Jones, a Negro, is in charge of the security effort. When the situation looks desperate, friction arises between Jones and Hardman over what is the best way of escaping the invaders. All but Jones are killed by the ghouls. In an ironic ending he dies when a member of a posse hunting the ghouls mistakes him for one of the flesh eaters and shoots him.

Streiner and Hardman produced the film effectively with a keen eye to boxoffice values. George A. Romero directed excitingly from a screenplay by John A. Russo marked with considerable skill.

The performances are good, with Jones and Hardman carrying the burden of the acting. Both are standouts.

CAST: Judith O'Dea, Duane Jones, Russell Streiner, Karl Hardman, Keith Wayne, Judith Ridley, Marilyn Eastman, Kyra Schon.

CREDITS: Produced by Russell Streiner and Karl Hardman; Directed by George A. Romero; Screenplay by John A. Russo; Cinematographer, George A. Romero.

—LOUS PELEGRINE

worked, shopped, or attended meetings or social functions all over southwestern Pennsylvania.

I wrote a news release and we mailed it with a "letter to the editor," to every daily and weekly newspaper listed in the Yellow Pages—which was roughly fifty newspapers. We enclosed the Image Ten press kit and several eight-by-ten still photos from our movie, which as I mentioned before, were printed en masse by Karl Hardman and Marilyn Eastman. Because of the local slant of "the first full-length motion picture filmed in Pittsburgh by a Pittsburgh company," almost every one of the fifty newspapers gave us extensive coverage, many of the weeklies printing my press release verbatim, accom-

panied by stills. Our actors and extras made a special effort to get themselves into their hometown newspapers. Some even were featured in college or industry publications. For instance, Mark Ricci, who had played one of our scientists in Washington, D.C., was the subject of an article in a Westinghouse Corporation newsletter.

Our philosophy was to play this as an "important movie" having its world premiere, instead of apologizing for it in any way because it was not what some might call a "serious drama" or an art film. Since this was showbiz, we might as well have the brass to go all the way with it as promoters and entrepreneurs.

NIGHT OF THE LIVING DEAD was scheduled to open on October 2, 1968 in twelve neighborhood and drive-in theaters in the Associated circuit, owned by George and Ernest Stern. We made a deal with the Sterns to take over the Fulton Theater, one of their classiest downtown houses, for our world premiere on the night of October first. This would be "by invitation only." Afterwards there would be a cocktail party at the William Penn Hotel, one of the best hotels in the city.

We took out a huge ad in the *Pittsburgh Press* announcing the premiere. We also had stylish invitations printed up for the critics, reporters, actors, investors, crew members, business associates, relatives and friends—about six hundred people—who would be asked to attend the special engagement. We worried—"What if three-quarters of them don't bother to show up?"—but this turned out to be an unnecessary worry. Nobody passed up the opportunity.

We went "first class" all the way. On the night of the premiere, a Tuesday, huge klieg lights shot their rotating beams into the sky as the principle cast and key production personnel, wearing tuxedos and evening gowns, arrived at the Fulton Theater in a fleet of limousines. We figured that some people might think this a bit much, others would be impressed, and still others would appreciate it as "high camp," even though we didn't intend it that way.

The theater was packed, since each person invited was permitted to bring a guest, and they all did. The audience response was nothing short of sensational. It was a great night for us. We got a standing ovation when the closing credits came on screen. The party afterwards was terrific.

But it still didn't necessarily prove much. We realized that it was one thing to get such an enthusiastic reaction from a select audience, and it would be another thing to get it from strangers. What if the general public didn't like our picture?

We thought that Continental's approach to the promotion of NIGHT OF THE LIVING DEAD tended to cheapen it—to not give it enough credit for being one of the better pictures in its genre—which we firmly believed that it was. One of the hoakier things that Continental did was to run an ad announcing that any theater patron who died of a heart attack while watching our movie would be covered by $50,000 worth of life insurance. The policy had been taken out through Lloyd's of London, so it actually existed, even though it was only a gimmick that no one could take seriously. And we thought it was of dubious value in promoting our movie.

Another interesting item is that, in some of the newspaper ads, the "nude ghoul" is not nude. For censorship reasons she had panties and a bra airbrushed onto her, even though only an aspect of her body would have been seen, and only from behind.

On the day after the premiere and cocktail party, we all showed up at The Latent Image and at Hardman Associates, even though we may have been a bit bleary-eyed. We hashed over the audience response, funny things that happened at the party, etc., while we tried to catch NIGHT OF THE LIVING DEAD promos on radio and TV, and clipped ads and articles out of newspapers.

Over the next few days, we started to drive around to the various theaters where our picture was playing, to see how the ticket sales seemed to be going, and to sit inobtrusively with the audiences. Every theater we checked out had a big crowd. All the reactions appeared to be very good. We began to get the idea that we may have at least some degree of success on our hands. But the big test for any picture is weekend business. What if the theaters didn't fill up on Friday, Saturday and Sunday? What if people would feel that they had better things to do on the weekend? What if they didn't choose to go to a drive-in in October—not exactly the warmest time of year for watching a movie from a car?

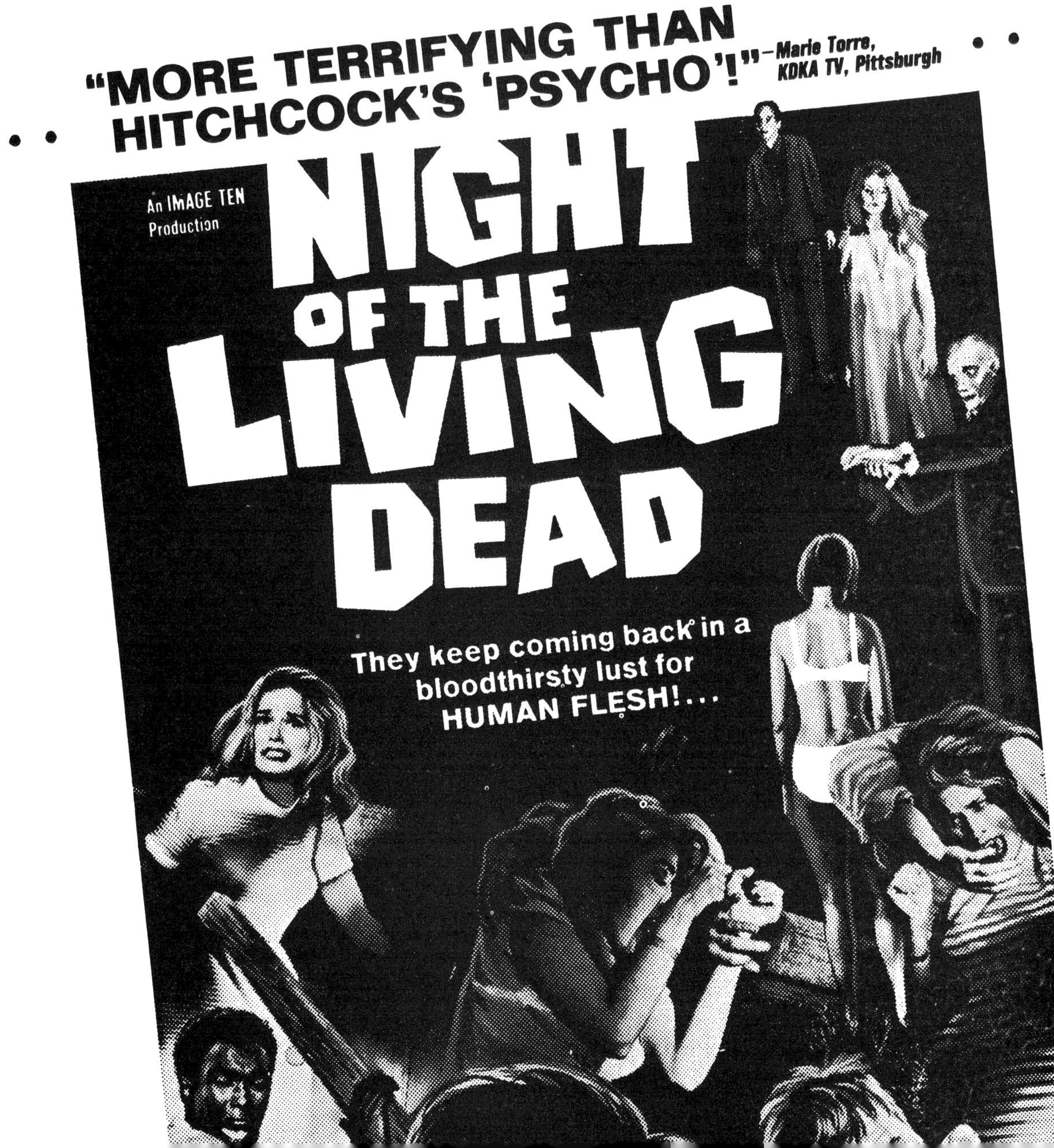

"MORE TERRIFYING THAN HITCHCOCK'S 'PSYCHO'!"—Marie Torre, KDKA TV, Pittsburgh

An IMAGE TEN Production

NIGHT OF THE LIVING DEAD

They keep coming back in a bloodthirsty lust for HUMAN FLESH!...

It turned out that *all* of the theaters were absolutely *packed.* Our picture was a *hit!* Some of the drive-ins actually had to turn cars away. For the first time in the history of the Associated circuit, George and Ernest Stern had to take out newspaper ads apologizing to the thousands of customers who didn't get in to see the feature attraction because there was no room.

Here are some excerpts from an article by Harold V. Cohen, entitled, MOVIE MADE HERE HITS THE JACKPOT:

It was Jerry Pickman on the phone, long-distance from New York. His voice was at practially fever pitch. "Those kids from Pittsburgh have really done it. They've hit the jackpot. It's a bonanza, a genuine gold-plated bonanza. If you don't believe me, call George Stern."

"You probably won't believe this," Mr. Stern said, "because I really have a hard time believing it myself, but NIGHT OF THE LIVING DEAD has been out-grossing anything we've had in a long time. For instance, the Memorial in McKeesport did $900 the entire week before it came in, and on last Saturday alone NIGHT OF THE LIVING DEAD did a fantastic $1,600. Take the Regent in East Liberty. Same thing. On Saturday it took in $1,700; I don't know when that theater has done that much in a single day. Not in years anyway. In every case, we're either holding the picture over or moving it to another house."

Did Mr. Stern think the fact that NIGHT OF THE LIVING DEAD was produced here in Pittsburgh, with a local cast, have anything to do with the spectacular business? Civic pride, perhaps?

"Not on your life," he insisted. "People don't spend their good money on something just because it has a local label. NIGHT OF THE LIVING DEAD has the kind of excitement audiences are going for these days. I'll make a prediction: it'll do the same kind of business everywhere."

Continental had no idea when they signed to distribute NIGHT OF THE LIVING DEAD that it would take off so spectacularly. "We figured," Mr. Pickman went on, "that it was a novelty that might make a good program filler and get us a few bucks...we never expected in our wildest dreams anything like this."

Russ Streiner working the clapstick

Well, to us, Jerry Pickman's comments proved what we had come to realize: that our distributor had undervalued our picture. By contrast, here are some comments of mine that appeared in the McKeesport *Daily News* on October 4, 1968, but were taken down in an interview with me before the picture even opened:

"Although the film is a fantasy-horror film, it is one of the best of its type. It has a lot of special effects, good acting, a logical script, and other good points that rank it above most of them. It's not for the squeamish, however."

George Stern's prediction turned out to be absolutely correct. NIGHT OF THE LIVING DEAD started to move from city to city, and kept on doing a booming business at the box office. It also began getting some glowing reviews. One of the earliest of these was from Louis Pelegrine, in *Film Daily*, October 21, 1968:

"...a pearl of a horror picture with all the earmarks of a sleeper. Accorded the right exploitation, it could make a whale of a showing. Those with queasy stomachs will find some of what goes on in the picture hard to take. Not many films have been able to create so vivid a sense of terror. There are a number of scenes that perhaps go too far in their realism."

This was the fun part of making a

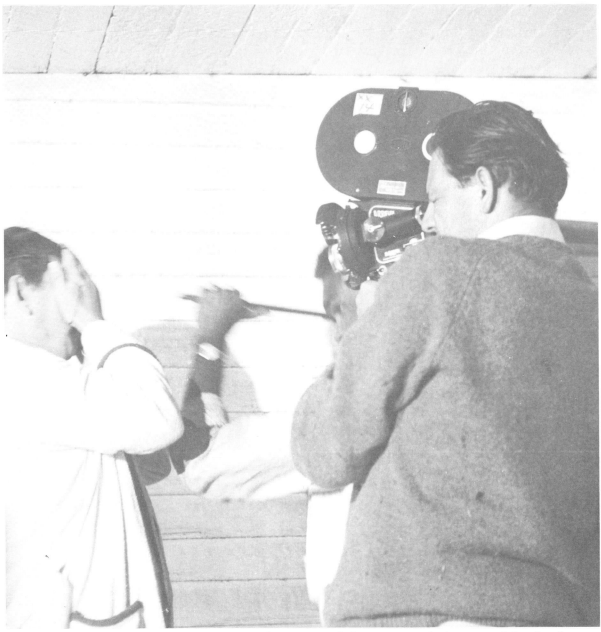

movie—basking in its success. But due to the exigencies of commercial jobs, George Romero was tied up and, unfortunately, could not fully enjoy the fruits of his labors on NIGHT OF THE LIVING DEAD. Once again, he had a slew of commercials to edit, for clients who insisted on having him and no one else because they considered him the bext editor in town. So Russ Streiner and I went to New York for the so-called "New York Premiere"—which was really only a small screening for the press at a Manhattan theater that was part of the Walter Reade chain.

Duane Jones, as one of the stars of our film, was on hand for the press screening. So were Jerry Pickman, Harold Marenstein and other executives from Continental. While coffee and donuts were being served in the theater lobby—which Russ and I thought were pretty shabby refreshments for a movie premiere—the reviewer from *Variety* charged over to Marenstein and Pickman and gave them a nasty tongue-lashing for, according to him, not treating the press with proper respect in the past, and not readily making their pictures available for previewing. This particular reviewer ended up writing one of the most devastating reviews NIGHT OF THE LIVING DEAD has ever gotten. Here are a few lines from it, which I find amusing in retrospect:

"This film casts serious aspersions on the integrity of its makers, distrib Walter Reade, the film industry as a whole, and exhibs who book the pic, as well as raising doubts about the future of the regional cinema movement and the moral health of filmgoers who cheerfully opt for unrelieved sadism.''

It went on and on, and didn't get any better. Of course we didn't see this review on the day of the press screening, but sometime later, and at the time it was dispiriting. But on that particular day in New York we enjoyed our status as young filmmakers with an apparent smash hit. Following the screening, Harold Marenstein, Jerry Pickman and Budd Rogers took us to lunch at a famous show-business restaurant, where we were joined by Diane Cilento, one of the stars of TOM JONES. At the time she was married to Sean Connery, and the Reade people pointed this out to us in case we didn't know, and also told us that they had made a deal to distribute her latest picture. All this was obviously designed to be

"heady stuff" for Russ, Duane and me, but I think we kept our heads on our shoulders and weren't overly snowed, considering our inexperience in these circles.

Budd Rogers, a ruddy, white-haired, grandfatherly sort of gentleman, gave us a friendly lecture on the way back to his office, that Russ afterwards joked was like Polonius's lecture to Laertes. Budd told us that we were going to hit it big and make a pile of money with our picture, and that we should invest it wisely and be shrewd, temperate young men. We were pleased to hear that he apparently believed in the picture so strongly, but we also figured that, after all our years of struggling and scrimping just to get by, if we *did* manage to get rich we deserved to blow some of our wealth on wine, women and song before settling down to being wise and temperate.

KEEPING THE BALL ROLLING: WE LAUNCH ANOTHER MOVIE

"LIVING DEAD is packing them in in Europe and the U.S., and this convinces the Latent Image people that they're onto something. 'We can compete with Hollywood at a fraction of the cost,' asserts George Romero, LIVING DEAD's 30-year-old director. He and his colleagues are hard at work on a second feature, a flick that should put that proposition to an eye-opening test. It's a youth-oriented picture, replete with hippies, generation gaps and several seductions. Mr. Romero boldly predicts his new film will gross between fifteen and thirty million dollars...if so, it would be another upward step in the heady six-year history of Latent Image, which before LIVING DEAD had ground out such industrial epics as THE CALGON STORY, KETCHUP, and HEINZ PICKLE NO. 1."

—Thomas Ehrich, The Wall Street Journal

Naturally, with the success of NIGHT OF THE LIVING DEAD, we got to talking right away about what our next picture should be. At first the leading candidate was something we referred to as the HORROR ANTHOLOGY, which we envisioned as a compendium of perhaps five vignettes that would be the most suspenseful, terrifying pieces ever committed to film.

But even though LIVING DEAD was earning plenty of money, none of it was immediately finding its way back into our pockets. We were learning yet another lesson in the dispiriting economics of the independent distribution system. It was taking the Reade Organizations months and months to collect from the theaters in which the picture had already played. And Reade didn't have the necessary capital to maximize the distribution impact. Either that, or they didn't have the will. In any case, they failed miserably at taking advantage of the "hot property" they obviously had on their hands. NIGHT OF THE LIVING DEAD had amply demonstrated that it had key-run potential. But its distribution remained sluggish, sporadic, lackadaisical. The hundreds of prints were never pulled and the heavy promotion was never launched that would have brought in millions of dollars more, and would have done it over a much shorter period of time.

So that left us chomping at the bit to make another feature, but with no clearcut way of financing it. Even if money *had* come back to us quickly, we would've had a problem using it, since Image Ten had been set up to produce only *one* picture and all the profits were allocated to the people who had worked on it. They would've had to vote unanimously to extend Image Ten's charter to do something new.

What we probably should have done was to start hitting one distributor after another, trying to find one who would back us financially. We tried this to some extent, but we didn't do enough of it. One of the reasons was that, even though a certain amount of fame was accruing to us as far as the movie fans and the motion picture industry were concerned, we were still in the position of having to devote most of our energy to commercial work to make a living. Another, and perhaps a primary, reason was that we liked the idea of making a good picture that we would *own*. We believed that our second time out of the gate we would make a real stunner and perhaps sell it to a major studio for a ton of money.

While we were tentatively discussing the HORROR ANTHOLOGY, I urged Rudy Ricci to write a different kind of script, just in case. Rudy had resigned his position with a major advertising agency to work full-time on his novel. So he had time to write, while George Romero and I were embroiled in a series of travel films for the state of Pennsylvania. Rudy wrote a very good screenplay entitled BEAUTY SLEEPING, about a lovely, intelligent young woman trapped in a stiflingly affluent, failing marriage. We submitted it to the Reade Organization, with a budget of over $300,000, and they turned it down for reasons that seemed strangely vague. I guess they didn't want to, or couldn't, come up with the money to back it. It was a big disappointment, especially for Rudy. The Reade Organization did go so far as to arrange the letter of credit for $50,000 that Russ Streiner alluded to in a previous chapter of this book. But they wanted the money to be used for a horror film, which would've been okay with us, except, as Russ said, they expected us to let them distribute it on the same terms as NIGHT OF THE LIVING DEAD, and we did not want to go along with that.

More and more, it was beginning to seem to us that we would once again have to find a way of raising production money, not from people in the movie business, but from independent investors. The spring of 1969 was rapidly approaching—the good shooting weather that we needed, and which wouldn't last too long—and we were not ready to roll with anything. We decided to put together a proposal for a motion picture production and try to raise $100,000 from local investors. The Latent Image would contribute facilities, equipment and services valued at another $100,000, for a total budget of $200,000.

In the meantime, several things had transpired to change our thinking away from the concept of the HORROR ANTHOLOGY. I had been leaning in another direction, anyway, from the time I urged Rudy Ricci to

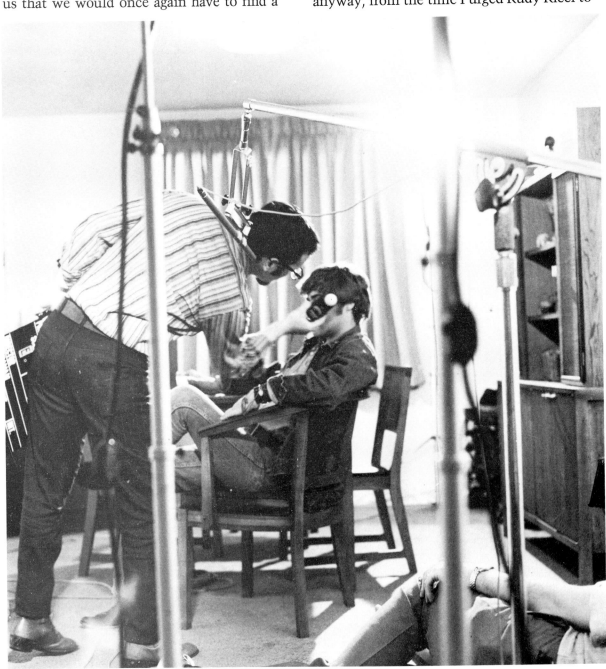

On one of many locations for AT PLAY WITH THE ANGELS

write the BEAUTY SLEEPING script. My feeling was that we ought to not only strike while the iron was hot, by making our second feature immediately, but that we also ought to make the type of picture that would prove to the industry and the public that our talents were not necessarily limited to the horror genre. George Romero seemed also to feel this way. One of the reasons was that we and everybody else connected with the movie business at that time could not help having our eyes on the success of THE GRADUATE, which had turned out to be the biggest-grossing film of 1968. It was the first of the vastly profitable ''youth-oriented'' pictures—like GOODBYE COLUMBUS, EASY RIDER, etc.—that would come to dominate the box-office in the late '60s and early '70s.

As it happened, our filmmaking group had a partially developed concept that seemed tailor-made for this trend. Even if such a movie managed to ride THE GRADUATE's coattails just a little bit, it could earn a lot of money. But we weren't going to aim only for a modest success and only in financial terms; we were going to try to make a picture that would be worthy of good reviews *and* would sell plenty of tickets. We wanted to make a key-run picture, not one that would play only drive-in and neighborhood theaters.

The ''partially developed concept'' that was to become our attempt at a youth-oriented picture first saw its existence as a half-hour film written by Rudy Ricci, directed by George Romero, and produced by The Latent Image, under the title of the RAY LAINE SCREEN TEST. It was exactly that: a screen test featuring our old friend Ray Laine, who had been a key man on the EXPOSTULATIONS project and had gone on to pursue an acting career on stage and in television. He was and is a fine actor. When he had made his screen test film, he had needed an actress to play opposite him, and Judith Ridley had been cast. There had been a special chemistry between them on screen. We were intrigued by it. Others were, too. The RAY LAINE SCREEN TEST won a Gold Medal in 1968 from the Visual Communications Society.

George Romero and I were convinced that this half-hour film could be embellished into a feature-length movie and, besides, it could be used as a promotional piece to help us raise investment for an expanded version. Furthermore, it wouldn't need to be an ''expansion'' in the strictest sense; it could be something new and dynamic that took its inspiration from the chemistry between, and the characters played by, Ray Laine and Judith Ridley in the SCREEN TEST. Most of our group agreed. Rudy Ricci had reservations, but nevertheless he started writing a new screenplay, while I began writing an investment brochure and Russ Streiner put together budget figures. The project initially became known by the working title that Rudy gave it: AT PLAY WITH THE ANGELS. Later it was changed to THERE'S ALWAYS VANILLA, and still later to THE AFFAIR.

We were stunned by how easy it was to raise the money we needed. This was primarily due to the success of NIGHT OF THE LIVING DEAD, but it was also due to the effectiveness of Russ Streiner, who pitched

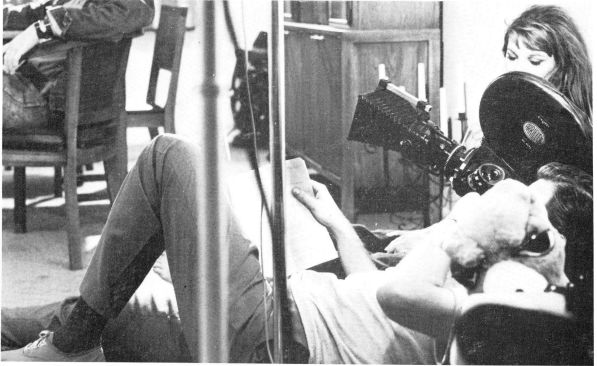

George Romero filming "At Play With the Angels"

103

most of the investors. Within a short time we had the $100,000.

We gave Karl Hardman and Marilyn Eastman an opportunity to be part of the AT PLAY WITH THE ANGELS enterprise, but they did not see the merit in the SCREEN TEST film that we at Latent Image saw, and so they decided not to get involved. So Russ Streiner and I were going to co-produce it, with George Romero directing from a screenplay by Rudy Ricci.

Now that it looked like we were going to be on our way again with a big, exciting project, and since we had it adequately funded—something new in our our purview—we decided to augment our staff so that the commercial end of the business could run smoothly while we worked on the feature. It was still important to us to show clients that we weren't about to neglect them just because we had suddenly become apparently successful as independent filmmakers.

We hired Cramer Riblett, an old friend of ours, as a commercial producer. Cramer had been in charge of the audio-visual department at the University of Pittsburgh, and had helped out on Latent Image's commercial jobs on numerous occasions over the years, chipping in on technical aspects and even appearing on film as an actor or model when the situation called for it. We felt good about finding ourselves in a position of being able to bring Cramer into our filmmaking group full-time.

On-camera for Channel 11 TV

104

We also hired Paul McCollough, who had studied journalism and filmmaking at Penn State. Paul worked as assistant cameraman on AT PLAY WITH THE ANGELS. Later, he wrote the original screenplay that formed the basis for George Romero's movie, THE CRAZIES. And he worked as cinematographer and editor on two of my pictures, THE BOOBY HATCH and MIDNIGHT.

So far, so good. Except, things immediately began to go wrong. For once, raising money had been the easy part, and now that we had it, our previously tight little group started to come unglued.

Why it fell apart would be a book in itself. Suffice it to say that, from the jump, there were internal arguments over the script, the concept, the cast, the production schedule, and the functions of key production personnel. Whereas, with NIGHT OF THE LIVING DEAD we had pulled together as one, now we were pulling in separate directions. This wasn't *entirely* the case, but it was enough to undermine the project. A movie eventually got made, but it was far from our best work. It also ran way over schedule and over budget. By the time we got it done, a glut of youth-oriented pictures had usurped the market, beating us to the punch. Our picture needed to have timeliness and innocent charm, and those qualities had been smothered and lost in the production squabbles and hassles.

The movie was still good enough to get sold and distributed by Cambist Films (distributors of a hit picture of that period, called CRY UNCLE), but it was not the success we had hoped for. Because of the production delays and additional time wasted in selling it and doping out a promotional campaign, it didn't come out until 1972. By that time, some further dissension had split our group apart. I say "split apart" in a business sense, because on a personal level we've remained friends. And some of us have worked together over the years on some movies. It was just that on AT PLAY WITH THE ANGELS we did not all see eye to eye, so that it seemed that the angels had deserted us for a while.

Pittsburgh Post-Gazette *Daily Magazine*

TUESDAY, OCTOBER 7, 1969

Latent Image Producing Its Second Feature Here

City to Be 'Hollywood on the Mon?'

Independent Firm Hopes For 2nd 'Hit'

By The Associated Press

HOLLYWOOD on the Monongahela? "Lights, camera, action" on Fort Pitt Boulevard?

You better believe it, Darryl Zanuck.

Pittsburgh, still trying to overcome its blue-collar image of smoke and steel—and not wholly succeeding—seems the least likely place to set up cinematic shop.

What other city, for instance, can offer poor weather, a lack of facilities, poor weather, inexperienced laboratory technicians, and poor weather?

Yet the Latent Image, a young, independent producing company, is taking advantage of great changes in the movie industry—mainly the demise of "big studio" domination—to test whether low-budget films produced in Pittsburgh can be successful.

★ ★ ★

IT STARTED about seven years ago when a handful of Pittsburgh-area collegians, mostly art students, decided to stick together after graduation and some "postgraduate" work in regional Pennsylvania theater. They began by producing commercials and educational and industrial films, mainly for local consumption.

Two years ago, they formed an offshoot company, Image Ten, to produce a feature film—between commercials, so to speak. They got some 30 investors interested—purely as a business venture—and filmed an admitted exploitation entry, a gory horror picture called "Night of the Living Dead," for $125,000.

Its national distributors are now projecting a box-office gross of $2.5 million by the end of the year, of which Image Ten can expect about $250,000 for 1969 only.

★ ★ ★

FOLLOW such a success? Only this

Judith Ridley and Ray Laine are 'on camera' as they run across Point State Park in a scene from "At Play with the Angels" being filmed here by a local group, The Latent Image.

Associated Press Photo

The production budget for the all-Pittsburgh-area color filming is $200,-000 and the story deals with contemporary youth, the "in" theme.

Russell W. Streiner, the company's tall, bespectacled, bookish-looking secretary-treasurer who serves as producer of "At Play With The Angels," . . . burgh is not the most . . . feature film

laboratory technicians and poor weather.

"We're really 'roughing' it here," he adds. "We're like pioneers. But we like it here. And, more importantly, we want to retain control."

★ ★ ★

THE POINT IS that when young, inexperienced filmmakers deal with major film companies, strong movie . . . and a big movie business at- . . . often have to give . . . as cameramen, lighting men, editors and such.

As a not-so-incidental sidelight, their feature film production has helped their TV commercial production as well. They well remember their fee for their first commercial: $150. For a recent one, they received $30,000.

With what Streiner calls the loosening climate in the film industry, they've been able to come a long way since the days they almost went broke . . . in the telephone book. film

WHAT NIGHT OF THE LIVING DEAD MEANS: TO ITS MAKERS AND TO ITS FANS

"Death in NIGHT OF THE LIVING DEAD is meaningless, total, inevitable. The monsters who live are not very much different from those destroyed. Romero's film is a bleak, relentless nightmare of our fears in which nothing can save us, in which we are trapped between the horror of death and life. That the film should have such broad appeal is a tribute to its skillful execution, but it also may mean that the very act of recognizing the hopelessness makes us better able to face its implications. Sitting through NIGHT OF THE LIVING DEAD is like an intensive session with a good psychiatrist. You come to grips with things you would often rather not face, but having faced them is, somehow, to lessen their ultimate horror."
—Stuart M. Kaminsky, Cinefantastique

Over the years, NIGHT OF THE LIVING DEAD has been a great source of pride and a career booster. The best proof that it was not "just a fluke" is that the key people behind the production have continued to do well in their chosen fields.

Karl Hardman and Marilyn Eastman are partners in Hardman-Eastman Associates, a booming enterprise, where they continue to write, produce, direct and star in radio and television productions, movies and industrial shows here and abroad.

Russell W. Streiner is director of broadcast production for a major advertising agency. His brother Gary is a producer for a commercial video production company in Boston.

Rudy Ricci recently won a gold medal in the Houston Film Festival for his screenplay, AT-TACK OF THE REAL DEAD PEOPLE, which he will soon produce as a movie. From the same festival, George Kosana won top prize for a script that he wrote, two years ago, so he has developed into quite an excellent writer as well as an actor.

Bill Hinzman is president of his own film production company. He will be producing a movie based on one of my books, THE MA-JORETTES.

Vince Survinski still works with George Romero and currently has a role in DAY OF THE DEAD. George, of course, has gone on to write and direct crowd-pleasing movies like MARTIN, CREEPSHOW and DAWN OF THE DEAD. I expect that DAY OF THE DEAD will also be a smash hit.

In my own case, when I wrote the noveliza-tion for NIGHT OF THE LIVING DEAD, which was published in 1974, it was the first step back into the career as a novelist that I had envisioned for myself, before getting into the movie business. I have not quit making movies, and to date have been involved in the writing, production and direction of four of them, including NIGHT OF THE LIVING DEAD, THE AFFAIR, THE BOOBY HATCH, and MIDNIGHT. But I have mostly been writing novels. The ninth one, DAY CARE, which deals with brain implants in gifted children, will be published in March of 1985, and will soon be followed by INHUMAN, a story of what can happen when the most bestial, primitive aspect of man's nature begins to control him. In the United States, most of my novels have been published by Pocket Books. They have also been published in about a dozen foreign countries.

With Russ Streiner and Rudy Ricci, I wrote a screenplay entitled RETURN OF THE LIV-ING DEAD, which was bought by Fox Films. It was subsequently revised and rewritten by Dan O'Bannon, the writer of ALIEN and BLUE THUNDER. O'Bannon then directed the picture, to be distributed by Hemdale overseas and by Orion in the United States, as a major release. I wrote the novelization.

So, our decision to make a low-budget "monster flick" has paid off in more ways than just financially. For those of us who chose to do so, it has enabled us to continue working as writers and filmmakers. It was our first step in the right direction. Since then, we've kept moving.

"FOR ONCE AN EXPLOITATION DOUBLE-BILL GIVES THE CUSTOMER HIS MONEY'S WORTH!"

LOS ANGELES
PACIFIC DRIVE-IN MULTIPLE
$157,420.00

NEWINGTON, CONN. 3 DAYS
$5,580.00
HARTFORD DRIVE-IN

LOUISVILLE, KY. PRESTON, DRIVE-IN
FIRST WEEK
$8,732.00
SECOND WEEK
$3,821.00
AND HELD OVER!

TROY, N.Y. PROCTOR THEATRE
$10,785.00
ONE WEEK

EL PASO PALACE
$17,500.00
3 WEEKS

AUGUSTA, GA.
$4,098.00
IMPERIAL DRIVE IN

HOUSTON ONE WEEK MULTIPLE
$22,000.00

NEW YORK
40 HOUSES MULTIPLE
$177,130.00
and HELD OVER

DAYTON, OHIO 3 HOUSES
$16,553.00

SCHENECTEDY STATE THEATRE
$8,425.00
ONE WEEK

DETROIT MULTIPLE ONE WEEK
$18,655.00

WATERTOWN, N.Y. 3 DAYS
$2,685.00
WATERTOWN DRIVE-IN

DES MOINES, IOWA ONE WEEK
$4,060.00
PIONEER DRIVE-IN

AUSTIN, TEXAS ONE WEEK
$9,592.00

DALLAS MULTIPLE—FIRST WEEK
$41,880.00
AND HELD OVER!

RAPID CITY, S.D. ELKS THEATRE
$4,399.00
ONE WEEK

MINNEAPOLIS FRAN AVENUE DRIVE IN 5 DAYS
$5,810.00
DURING BLIZZARD AND ZERO WEATHER

SAN FRANCISCO
$28,282.00
MULTIPLE—FIRST WEEK

WACO, TEXAS CIRCLE DRIVE-IN
$3,354.00
ONE WEEK

BOSTON MULTIPLE
FIRST WEEK
$68,500.00

CHICAGO
MULTIPLE—FIRST WEEK
$110,580.00

CLEVELAND MULTIPLE
$37,000.00

HONOLULU WAIALAI THEATRE
$6,251.00
ONE WEEK

NEW HAVEN
$6,431.00
ONE WEEK

PITTSBURGH MULTIPLE
$75,874.00
ONE WEEK and HELD OVER

PHILADELPHIA MULTIPLE ONE WEEK
$80,120.00

MILFORD, CONN. ONE WEEK
$5,389.00
MILFORD DRIVE-IN

ALBANY PALACE THEATRE
$11,038.00
ONE WEEK

In the meantime, besides enjoying immense popularity all over the world, and remaining constantly in release since its premiere, NIGHT OF THE LIVING DEAD has come to be known as a "cult film." Here is the definition of *cult* from my desk dictionary:

"cult (kult) n. 1. A system of religious rites and observances. 2. Zealous devotion to a person, ideal, or thing. 3. The object of this devotion. 4. The followers of a cult."

Somehow, when I think of a NIGHT OF THE LIVING DEAD cult, I conjure up images of hooded figures gathering in a dark cemetery to watch the picture projected on a tombstone. This kind of extreme would suit the dictionary definition. I'm not sure that fans of a horror movie need to be called a "cult" any more than do fans of a mainstream movie like CITIZEN KANE. In fact, labeling them with that terminology is a way of belittling them for greatly enjoying a picture in a genre that

Clairton extras, Ray Russo, Geno Ratkiewicz & Ken Croyle

many people do not sufficiently respect.

NIGHT OF THE LIVING DEAD played for a year and a half in the largest theater in Madrid. It also played for a year and a half in Rome. But its so-called "cult" reputation came mostly from its long run in midnight screenings at the Waverly Theater in Greenwich Village. It stayed there for about two years, and kept on attracting huge crowds. During the early part of that run, in the spring and summer of 1971, it got glowing reviews from Rex Reed and Howard Smith, and also an article in the New York *Daily News* that stuck it with the "cult" label:

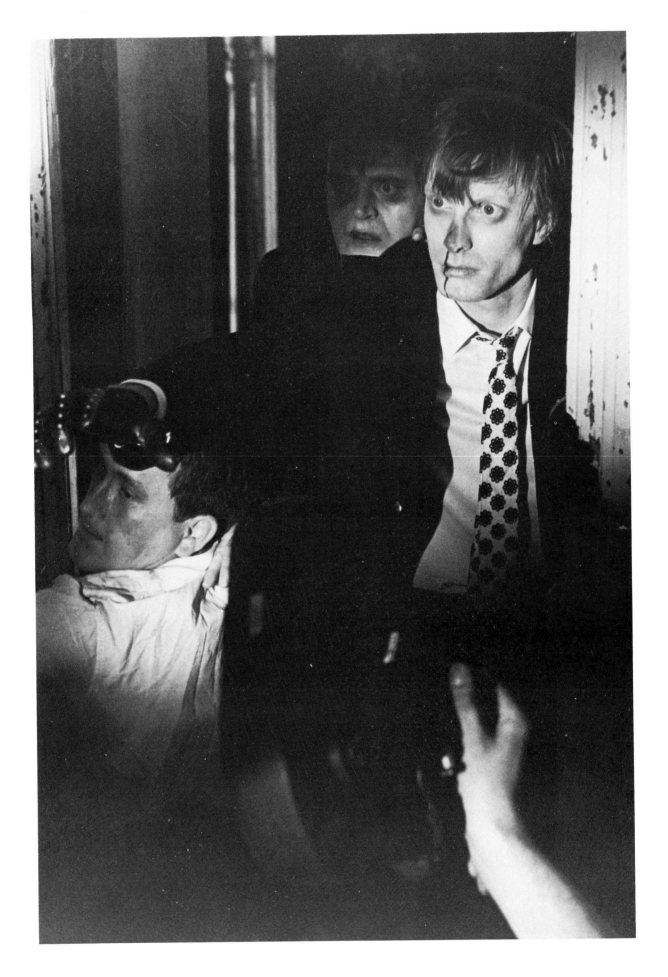

"Every Friday and Saturday night for the last month, a line of eager, smiling young faces has stretched along the block in front of Greenwich Village's Waverly Theater, waiting with restrained impatience to be admitted for the midnight showing of a horror movie called THE NIGHT OF THE LIVING DEAD. The film already had acquired a nucleus of a cult, for when it was shown last year in a series at the Museum of Modern Art, people had to be turned away."

—Ernest Leogrande, New York Daily News

I wonder if the hordes of people who had to be turned away from the theaters when NIGHT OF THE LIVING DEAD opened in Pittsburgh were part of this "cult." Or were they just part of the "silent majority" alluded to in this review from a British publication called *Sight and Sound*?

"Who are these ghouls, who are these saviours, all of them so horrifying, so convincing, who mow down, defoliate and gobble up everything in their path? In the film a local TV station sends out a warning message: 'The ghouls are ordinary people...but in a kind of trance.' (Indeed, some of them are just little old ladies in tennis shoes and runny make-up.) Many of these ordinary people, in all the trance-like security of their 'silent majority' can be seen these days...cramming their popcorn in front of a large Broadway screen where Fox's PATTON is doing land-office business."

—Elliott Stein

I personally believe that some critics have a tendency to read a bit much into the creations they are studying, in their zeal to find messages and "hidden meanings." One reviewer who absolutely detested NIGHT OF THE LIVING DEAD wrote that if President Lyndon Johnson had gone to see enough such "cheap, bloody movies" he might have obtained a sufficient release of his pent-up emotions that he wouldn't have needed to "get off on" the napalming of the Vietnamese.

Repeating myself for the sake of this dis-cussion, I think that what is fundamental about NIGHT OF THE LIVING DEAD is that it is a solid, logical story within the context of its fictional premise. This comes across strongly, despite its budget limitations. It enables people to suspend disbelief. They find themselves emotionally affected by it—in fact, *scared* by it. Then they start trying to analyze *why* they had such an atavistic, visceral reaction. Sometimes they find reasons that the filmmakers never consciously intended.

Kyra Schon eating normal food between takes

This is because a *believable* picture only attains believability when it adequately mirrors what people call *reality*—in other words, what *feels* real in their own lives. NIGHT OF THE LIVING DEAD manages to feel real enough to inspire real terror, real dread. Therefore, for many of us, it serves as a useful vehicle to enable us to confront and perhaps temporarily subdue the terror and dread in our daily lives.

Not long after NIGHT OF THE LIVING DEAD came out, Sam Peckinpah directed a movie called STRAW DOGS that terrified people much in the same way, and elicited similar analyses from critics. I read an interview with Peckinpah where he said that he was handed a bad novel and he was handed a screenwriter, and the only thing he could find

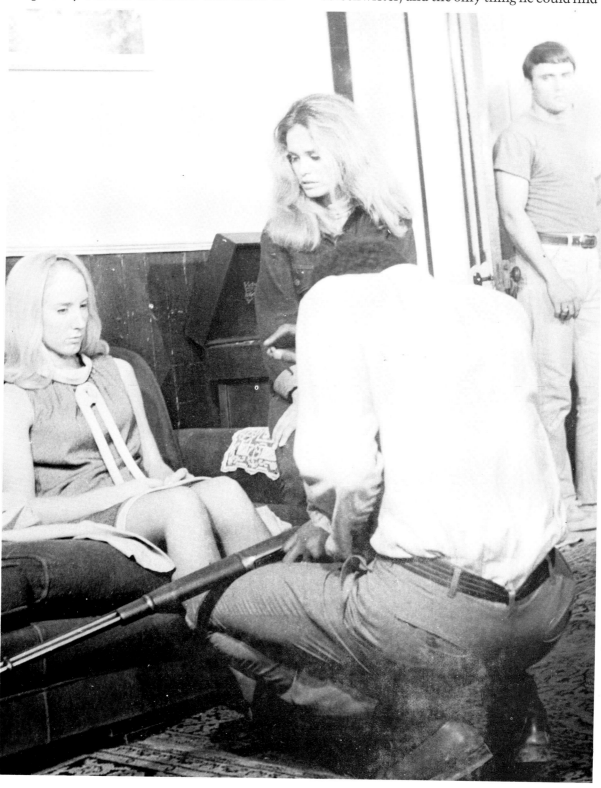

good in the novel was the action in the siege at the end. So he decided to keep that and make the most he could out of it, and do a good action story. The siege of the mindlessly hateful townspeole in the last half hour of STRAW DOGS reminded me very much of the final siege of the ghouls in NIGHT OF THE LIVING DEAD. Millions of filmgoers were terrified by both depictions of the onslaught of the mindless against the competent, the empathetic. It is clear that all of us must have a deepseated fear of being set upon, attacked, by unfeeling, uncaring personages who do not take the time to know and respect, but only to hate us. We all dread the witch hunters, the lynch mob, the terrorists who plant bombs to kill those they have never met. The existence of this primal fear, this dread, within our psyches, and its vivid evocation, is the truly basic reason for the success of NIGHT OF THE LIVING DEAD.